# | blessed |
# Assurance

# | blessed |

# Assurance

The Grace and Glory of Romans 8

John Miller

Blessed Assurance



Published by:
Revival Christian Fellowship
29220 Scott Road
Menifee, CA 92584
www.revival.tv

ISBN: 979-8-9960216-0-4

Cover Design: Elizabeth Arriaga
Layout: Elizabeth Arriaga
Editors: Steve Halliday and Terri Villines
Copyeditors: Aaron Rugh and Hayley McDonald

Printed in the United States of America

"To Jesus Christ in whom there is no condemnation, and in Him no separation. Be all praise and glory."

"For you did not receive the spirit of bondage again to fear, but you received the Spirit of adoption by whom we cry out, "Abba, Father." The Spirit Himself bears witness with our spirit that we are children of God, and if children, then heirs—heirs of God and joint heirs with Christ, if indeed we suffer with Him, that we may also be glorified together."

— Romans 8:15-17 (NKJV)

# CONTENTS


The Greatest Chapter in the Bible 1

No Condemnation 5

A New Liberation 23

Life in the Spirit 39

Adopted Into God's Family 57

Groaning for Glory 73

God's Providential Care 91

Salvation's Golden Chain 109

Blessed Assurance 125

NOTES 143

## Introduction

# THE GREATEST CHAPTER IN THE BIBLE

Many Bible scholars call Romans 8 the greatest chapter in the whole Bible. Someone once compared Scripture to a ring, with Romans 8 as the diamond setting in the center of that ring. It's the sparkling jewel of our preservation in Christ.

In this book, we're going to dive into Romans 8 to learn how safe we are in the arms of Jesus. That amazing chapter opens with "no condemnation . . . in Christ" and ends with no separation "from the love of God which is in Christ Jesus our Lord."

Romans 8 is Paul's magnificent summary of how God saves sinners.

## GET READY TO TRANSFORM YOUR LIFE

I believe that a better understanding and application of the truths found in Romans 8 will transform your Christian life. As God's Spirit works through God's Word, a revolutionary change will take place in your life.

You will learn that you are safe in the arms of Jesus, that the Spirit has come to direct your life, and that in Christ, you can fulfill all the demands of the law.

Allow me to set the stage for what's ahead by briefly rehearsing the context of the eighth chapter of Romans. Notice that in Christ:

- We have a new assurance of victory (Romans 8:1-13)
- We have a new assurance of sonship (8:14-17)
- We have a new assurance of hope (8:18-25)
- We have a new assurance of help because the Holy Spirit helps us in our infirmities, even interceding for us in prayer (8:26-30)
- We have a new assurance of security because we are kept by the power of God unto the day of redemption (8:31-39)

You see it all there: no condemnation, no separation, and in between, no defeat.

## WHO CAN BE AGAINST YOU?

Someone once described Romans 8 like this: "God is for you, Christ is around you, and the Spirit is in you." No wonder Paul cried out, "If God be for us, who can be against us?"

This book focuses on the blessed assurance that every believer has in Christ. *Blessed Assurance* is for *all* those who are in Christ! Whether you came to faith in Jesus many years ago or you're still wondering whether

Jesus is for you, I hope and pray that as you read what follows, you will come to say, as Paul did,

"In all these things we are more than conquerors through Him who loved us" (Romans 8:37).

# 1

# NO CONDEMNATION

> *There is therefore now no condemnation to those who are in Christ Jesus.*
>
> - *Romans 8:1*

Just before we start to unpack that thrilling message, let's take a very short dip into what scholars call "textual criticism."

## WHERE DOES IT BELONG?

In the King James version, verse 1 continues, "who walk not after the flesh, but after the Spirit." The older manuscripts omit that portion from verse 1 but instead include it in verse 4, where it fits much better contextually.

In fact, the phrase simply doesn't belong in verse 1. It's an interpolation, accidentally put there by a scribe centuries ago. We know from the most ancient manuscripts we have that this is the case. We can trust our Bibles!

We have a multitude of manuscript evidence to determine which verses go where. If the portion quoted above did belong in verse 1, it would almost certainly contradict what Paul says there—that in Christ, there is no condemnation. The apostle gives us no condition for "no condemnation," other than being in Christ. Paul does not mean that God won't condemn you so long as you walk in the Spirit. He insists that God won't condemn you because *you are in Christ*. If you are in Christ, there is no condemnation. That's the only condition. We should therefore read verse 1 like this: "There is therefore now no condemnation to those who are in Christ Jesus."

And now, we're ready to unpack the astonishing promise found in the very first verse of Romans 8.

## WORD ONE: "THEREFORE"

Let's look at four important words or phrases in verse one. The first word to consider is "therefore," as in, "There is *therefore* now no condemnation . . . ."

The word "therefore" indicates that Paul is summing up what he has already written in the book of Romans. Whenever you see a "therefore" in Scripture, you ought to ask what it's there for. The question for us here is, how far back does the "therefore" extend?

From chapter 1 to chapter 7, Paul describes humankind's condemnation, salvation, and sanctification. In Romans 1:18 to 3:20, humanity is seen under the wrath of God and subject to His condemnation. Romans 3:19 says, "that all the world may become guilty before God." That's the end of that first section, where every mouth is stopped. The religious person, the Jewish individual, the heathen—everyone in the world stands condemned and guilty before God.

Paul then moves into a section about salvation, which describes how God saves sinners in Christ Jesus. From Romans 3:21 all the way through chapter 5, Paul talks about how God justifies the condemned. Justification is the opposite of condemnation. So, the apostle shows us how we're first condemned and then how we're justified or declared righteous.

In Romans 6-7, we see the believer's sanctification.

And then, in chapter 8, Paul wants to consider man's preservation. Romans 8 is the summit, the mountain peak, of Scripture. The book of Romans is Paul's theological last will and testament. He takes everything he knows about how God saves sinners from the gospel and puts it into this marvelous book.

Romans moves from condemnation to justification to sanctification to preservation, or how God keeps us safe in Jesus Christ. God saves us in Christ Jesus. In Christ Jesus, we are justified, sanctified, and glorified. Salvation has three tenses: past, present, and future.

In the past tense, we *have been* saved; God has justified us and declared us righteous. This is our position in Christ. Our standing is complete in Jesus. Justification is not a process but is complete the moment you are born again. Your standing will never change. You are righteous in Christ.

In the present tense, we *are being* saved. This is the process of sanctification, a lifelong progression of being changed to become increasingly like Jesus Christ.

In the future tense, we *will be* glorified. This will happen when we go to be with Jesus, whether by death or through the Rapture, and we get a new, supernatural body. Praise God!

So then, God *has* justified us, He *is* sanctifying us, and one day He *will* glorify us.

I am convinced that once a person is justified, glorification is a sure thing. What begins in grace ends in glory. Those who have been justified *will* be glorified, so don't fret. Don't freak out or worry, "Am I going to make it to heaven? Am I going to get in just by the skin of my teeth?" If you have placed your faith in Jesus for salvation, you have been declared righteous in Christ. You're being made holy in Christ. And one day, you will be glorified in Christ.

Donald Grey Barnhouse said, "It is my measured opinion that confusing sanctification with justification is the cause of more false doctrine than any other error that has ever been committed by religious thinkers."[1] I agree with him.

Many Christians cause themselves unnecessary problems, because after they get saved, they expect to be perfect right away. And because they're not perfect immediately but instead falter and stumble, they imagine that they've lost their salvation. They worry that God has kicked them out of His family, that they're not going to go to heaven, or that they must work harder to stay saved. They imagine that God is angry with them. They fail to understand that they are positionally righteous before God as a settled, divine *fact*.

If you are a Christian, *you have been justified*. There is no such thing as different degrees of being justified. There are, however, different degrees of sanctification on this earth. Some Christians really do live a more holy, godly life than others.

The words "saint," "sanctified," and "holy" all come from the same root word in Greek, which means to be "set apart and made holy." Some Christians do, in fact, live a more sanctified life than others; they've grown in their walk with the Lord. They live a more Christ-like life. They're more Spirit-filled. And so, they're more like Jesus.

Other Christians have a much longer way to go! Does that describe you? Maybe you've been a Christian for a long time, but still feel like you'll never measure up.

Don't forget that sanctification is a process that will never end until we get to heaven. So, remember: salvation is positional, practical, and then it's perfect. Think of it like this:

Justification = position

Sanctification = practice

Glorification = perfection

This is foundational to understanding what it means to be in Christ, to be under no divine condemnation. Verse 1 of Romans 8 summarizes not only the whole of that chapter, but the whole of the book of Romans and even the whole Bible. It encapsulates how God saves sinners.

He saves us *in Christ Jesus*.

## WORD TWO: "NOW"

When does the blessing of salvation come to us? God answers with a single word: *now*.

This is a time word. It points to the change that comes into the life of an individual who has been justified in Christ.

Since Paul began with, "Therefore there is no condemnation," we might well ask him, "*when* is there no condemnation, Paul?" And the apostle answers, "Now."

The moment a sinner is saved, his or her condemnation is removed. *Now* we are justified. Justification happens the instant we believe and trust in Jesus Christ and are born again. Second Corinthians 5:17 says, "Therefore, if anyone is in Christ, he is a new creation; old things have passed away; behold, all things have become new."

You *were* under condemnation, but now you are saved in Christ. Justification is a believer's present possession. Those "in Christ" have it right now, at this moment, and they will never again face any condemnation, *ever*.

## WORD THREE: "NO CONDEMNATION"

The third "word" (or phrase) in verse 1 is "*no condemnation*." Paul started with "therefore," added "now," and then immediately moved to "no condemnation."

The word "no" in the original Greek is emphatic. English doesn't feature such a distinction. When we say "no" in English, it's just no. For emphasis, we must yell or scream, or pound on something. But ancient Greek featured a couple of words for "no." The word here is an emphatic "no." It means "No way!"

In the original text, the "no" appears at the front of the sentence to emphasize its importance, like this: "No condemnation therefore to those who are in Christ Jesus." In ancient Greek, the first word in a sentence is always the one most strongly emphasized.

Paul considers the wicked, sinful, lost, condemned human race and then says of those who are born again and placed in Christ that they stand under no condemnation—not now, not ever, not at any point in the distant future. There will never be condemnation for those who have placed their faith in Jesus: "*NO* condemnation therefore to those who are in Christ Jesus." What a glorious, magnificent truth!

When Paul writes in Romans 5:1 about the blessings and benefits of being saved or justified, he writes, "Having been justified by faith, we have peace with God through our Lord Jesus Christ." We have no condemnation because we're justified, and now we have peace with God because we've been forgiven in Jesus Christ.

Note that Paul says, "no condemnation," not "no sins" or "no mistakes." He doesn't say, "there is now therefore no stumbling of those who are in Christ." Why not? Because we *do* stumble. As Christians, we still sin. If you say you don't sin, you're a liar, and the truth is not in you (1 John 1:10). All of us sin.

Jesus said that if you have anger in your heart toward someone, you've murdered them. Some of us murder others even on the way to church. Somebody cuts you off in traffic, and you sputter, "That idiot!" A little boy once asked his mother, "Mommy, why is it that when Dad drives, all the idiots come out?" The idiots didn't come out when Mom drove, only when Dad took the wheel.

We all stumble. We all sin. The Bible doesn't say, "There is now therefore no sins to those who are in Christ." We have wonderful days when we're walking in the Spirit and growing in sanctification, and other darker days or weeks when we stumble a lot, and our progress in sanctification takes a back seat. During those times, don't forget that *your position never changes*. You have the righteousness of Christ. Always keep in mind the distinction between your position and your practice.

Christians do sin. Believers in Jesus make moral mistakes. David, a man after God's own heart, committed adultery with Bathsheba and then had her husband killed to cover his sexual sin. Peter pulled his sword in the Garden of Gethsemane and tried to take off a servant's head. Abraham sinned. Moses sinned. All of God's greatest saints have stumbled and taken a fall.

So then, what does "no condemnation" mean? It means that God has acquitted you of guilt and has lifted the judicial sentence under which you were formerly held guilty. God has acquitted you and lifted His divine sentence.

Divine condemnation involves two things: first, it pronounces you guilty; and second, it delivers judgment appropriate to your guilt. In our criminal court systems, once you are found guilty, you enter the punishment or penalty phase. Divine condemnation means both things: you're found guilty, which brings punishment. The Bible says, "The wages of sin is death" (Romans 6:23).

Under Adam, we are under condemnation, but when we are born again, God takes us out of Adam and places us in Christ. The result? No condemnation!

If you are "in Christ," God does not condemn you now and never will. God is not angry with you. God will not kick you out of His family when you stumble and fall.

Someone will try to condemn you, however. Satan is rightly called the accuser of the brethren (Revelation 12:10). Some people also will try to condemn you, pointing their finger at you and putting you down. Even your own heart will try to condemn you (1 John 3:20).

But God will never condemn you!

Paul writes, "If God is for us, who can be against us?" (Romans 8:31). What a great question! If God is for us—and He is—then who can be against us? Three verses later, Paul adds, "Who is he who condemns? It is Christ who died, and furthermore is also risen, who is even at the right hand of God, who also makes intercession for us."

God does not condemn you. God will not kick you out of His family. God doesn't hate you. He may chasten you for your sin to bring you back into alignment with your true position and to help you grow in sanctification, but He will never kick you out of His family, judge you, or condemn you. All of that was firmly and finally dealt with at the Cross.

## WORD FOUR: "IN CHRIST JESUS"

A final word/phrase appears in verse 1, the most important in the verse: *"in Christ Jesus."*

I wish there were some way for me to fully communicate the ultimate importance of this concept. I believe it is the greatest truth taught in the Bible for believers to grasp.

Paul used the phrase more than a hundred times, making it his favorite statement in his epistles. Some say that the apostle used the phrase "in Christ" at least 165 times, whether in the form "in Christ," "in Christ Jesus," or "in Christ Jesus our Lord." Take time to read Ephesians 1 and note all the blessings from God that come to us because we are "in Christ Jesus." *All* the heavenly blessings of the Spirit come to us because we are "in Christ."

Exert the effort it takes to better understand what it means to be "in Christ." The only condition for no condemnation is being "in Christ Jesus."

Spiritually speaking, only two classes of humanity exist. There are those who are "in Christ," who experience no condemnation, and there are those "in Adam," who are condemned already and living under the wrath of God (Romans 5:12-21).

The two classes are not male/female. They're not race or nationality. They're not about education or social status. You're either "in Adam" or "in Christ."

Remember when Adam and Eve sinned in the Garden of Eden (Genesis 3)? Sin and death came upon them and through them to the whole human race. When Adam and Eve disobeyed in the Garden, they plunged all of humanity into sin and condemnation.

Everything that is true of Adam is also true of us. Every human being born into this world is born "in Adam." That is why we must be born again of the Spirit. Only in that way can we be taken out of Adam and born into Christ. Everyone born in Adam is under condemnation, but everyone born of the Spirit has been given salvation in Christ. Everything true of Christ is imputed to those "in Christ."

We could call these two classes of humanity "the saved" and "the unsaved." We could call them "believers" and "unbelievers." We could call them "Christians" and "non-Christians." But there is no in-between. There are believers and unbelievers, saved and unsaved, the lost and the found. No one is either half-saved or half-condemned. Think of it like this:

In Adam = condemned

In Christ = saved

This is not a popular view today! Many voices insist there are multiple paths to God, many roads to heaven, and all religions bring salvation. But you won't find that false idea in the Bible! Scripture is very simple: there is only one way to be saved, and that's in Christ Jesus. If you're not in Christ, then you're in Adam—and in that case, you're under sin, death, and condemnation.

I don't know how I can better emphasize the crucial importance of understanding what it means to be in Christ.

## SOME CRUCIAL QUESTIONS

Let's ask a few questions about being in Christ Jesus.

- How do you get "in Christ"?

You get "in Christ" by being born again, by believing in Jesus Christ as your Savior, through faith. You trust Him for your eternal salvation. Paul wrote, "For by grace you have been saved through faith, and that not of yourselves; it is the gift of God, not of works, lest anyone should boast" (Ephesians 2:8-9). When you put your trust in Him, the Spirit of God takes you out of Adam and places you in Christ.

Then it's the Holy Spirit's job to guide and direct you. Romans 8 describes life in the Spirit. In Romans 7, the Holy Spirit is mentioned once, but in Romans 8, He's mentioned repeatedly. We go from life in the flesh to life in the Spirit. God's Holy Spirit indwells you.

Paul told the believers in Corinth, "For by one Spirit we were all baptized into one body . . . and have all been made to drink into one Spirit" (1 Corinthians 12:13). It is the Holy Spirit's job not only to convict you of sin, regenerate you, and seal you unto the day of redemption, but He takes you out of Adam and transfers you into Christ so that you are identified with Him. That's the work of the Holy Spirit.

- Who is in Christ?

The Bible makes it crystal clear that *all* those who have submitted themselves to Christ through faith are truly in Christ. All those who have been born again—and only those who have been born again—are in Christ.

You can't be in Christ if you have never been born again. You *must* be born again to be in Christ, and if you are in Christ, then you're a Christian and a child of God.

There are no degrees of being in Christ. Remember the three tenses of salvation? We *have been* justified, we *are being* sanctified, and we *will be* glorified.

There are no degrees of justification. The moment you are born again, you are justified. Twenty, thirty, forty, fifty, sixty, or seventy years later, you are no more or less justified than you were the moment you trusted Jesus Christ. You cannot be less justified or more justified; you're just justified.

Some like to take the word "justified" and break it down to "just as if I'd never sinned." In justification, God is declaring you righteous. That's your eternal position or standing.

Our problem comes with our sanctification, where there *can* be degrees of holiness. We know this because there come times when we're *not* growing and becoming more holy, even though God says, "Be holy as I am holy" (Leviticus 11:44; 1 Peter 1:16). To be sanctified means to be made holy. Remember that the English words "saint," "sanctified," and "holy" all come from the same Greek root word, which means to be "set apart" and "made holy." We're positionally holy in Christ; we're being made practically holy by submitting to the Holy Spirit, and we will be made perfectly holy when we leave this world and get a new body.

- When do you get in Christ?

This is an easy one. You get in Christ the moment you get saved or regenerated.

- How long will you be in Christ?

As I read Scripture, I believe the answer is "forever." Once you're in Christ, you're always in Christ. Did you put yourself in Christ? No. And neither can you take yourself out of Christ. The Holy Spirit put you in Christ, and He's not going to take you out of Christ.

The Bible says you were bought at a price (1 Corinthians 6:20; 7:23). Once you're in Christ, you're always in Christ. That's why I've called this book *Blessed Assurance*.

Frankly, good Christians can and do disagree on this issue. Throughout history, this question has sparked a lot of arguments and debates. Some believe that you can lose your salvation. I don't know how anyone can study Romans 8—which starts with "no condemnation," in the middle is no defeat, and ends with no separation—and think that someone who is genuinely saved could ever be lost. The more I study this question, the more convinced I become that once you're in Christ, you're in Christ forever. I think the hymn writer Fannie Crosby had it exactly right:

> Blessed assurance, Jesus is mine!
>
> Oh, what a foretaste of glory divine!
>
> Heir of salvation, purchase of God,
>
> born of His Spirit, washed in His blood.
>
> This is my story, this is my song,
>
> praising my Savior all the day long.

This is my story, this is my song,

praising my Savior all the day long.

– Fannie Crosby, "Blessed Assurance, Jesus is Mine!"

Of course, I'm not perfect. Some people wrongly think that Pastor John Miller glows in the dark. Individuals have come up to my wife and said, "It must be awesome living with Pastor John." She usually says, tongue firmly in cheek, "Oh, yeah. It's *awesome*."

I've been justified, and I'm being sanctified, but I have a long way to go! And so do you. One day, however, all Christians will get to heaven, and on that day, we're all going to look at each other and say, "Isn't God good? Isn't the grace of God amazing?"

Every one of us is saved by grace. Every one of us is sanctified by grace. And one day, every one of us will be glorified by God's marvelous grace.

How long will we be in Christ? Romans 8:39 says that there is no separation "from the love of God which is in Christ Jesus our Lord." The Bible teaches that "you were sealed with the Holy Spirit of promise" until "the day of redemption" (Ephesians 1:13-14; 4:30).

The instant you are saved, you are sealed with the Spirit, which makes you secure until the day that you go home to be with Jesus Christ. *This* is your position. *This* is your standing. It's not progressive; it's perfect. It's your position in Christ!

## JESUS CHRIST, THE ARK OF OUR SALVATION

We all know of the story of Noah and the ark, when God brought judgment on the whole world (Genesis 6). I believe the Bible teaches that the flood was universal. Everyone on the earth, except Noah, his wife, his three sons, and their wives (and the animals on the ark), died in that worldwide flood.

Noah escaped because God had him build an ark. The Old Testament says that Noah was instructed to use pitch on the ark, both inside and out. The same Hebrew word translated "pitch" in Genesis 6:14 is translated "atonement" or "covering" in about 100 other places in the Old Testament. Henry Morris writes in *The Genesis Record*,

> The word for "pitch" (Hebrew kopher) is different from that used in other places in the Old Testament. It is equivalent to the Hebrew kaphar ("to cover") and, in the noun form, means simply a "covering."
>
> However, it is also the regular Hebrew word for "atonement," as in Leviticus 17: 11, for example. In essence, therefore, this is the first mention of "atonement" in the Bible. Whatever the exact nature of this "pitch" may have been, it sufficed as a perfect covering for the Ark, to keep out the waters of judgment, just as the blood of the Lamb provides a perfect atonement for the soul.[2]

Noah's ark gives us a type or picture of Jesus Christ. This big boat had just one door and only one way in. Noah and his family went through the open door, along with all the animals. God then shut the door. Only then did the rains come down and the flood come up. Who was saved? Only those in the ark.

Jesus Christ is our ark of safety. There is no condemnation for those who are in the ark of Christ. The world will be judged and condemned, but Christians have passed from death to life.

Jesus said, "Most assuredly, I say to you, he who hears My Word and believes in Him who sent Me has everlasting life, and shall not come into judgment [or condemnation], but has passed from death into life" (John 5:24). All those who hear God's Word and believe on Jesus pass from death to life.

Jesus said again, "My sheep hear My voice, and I know them, and they follow Me. And I give them eternal life, and they shall never perish; neither shall anyone snatch them out of My hand. My Father, Who has given them to Me, is greater than all; and no one is able to snatch them out of My Father's hand" (John 10:27-29).

It's almost as though Jesus has taken a nail and driven it through the boards. He turns it over and bends the head of the nail down, so no one can take it out. "I give them eternal life. They shall never perish. No one can pluck them out of My hand. My Father, Who gave them to Me, is greater than all. No one can pluck them out of My Father's hand."

Some might ask, "Does that mean we can live however we want and still expect to go to heaven? Because I'm saved, can I go out and sin as much as I please?" The answer is obviously "No!"

When you became a Christian, God removed your condemnation and liberated you. Romans 8:2-4 begins, "For the law of the Spirit of life [a reference to the Holy Spirit] in Christ Jesus has made me free from the law of sin and death." We begin right there: Justification has freed us from the condemnation and guilt of the law. "For what the law could not do in that it was weak through the flesh, God did by sending His own Son in the likeness of sinful flesh, on account of sin: He condemned sin in the flesh."

Paul continues, "that the righteous requirement of the law might be fulfilled in us who do not walk according to the flesh but according to the Spirit [our sanctification]."

Being in Christ and thus freed from divine condemnation is no license to live sinfully. God plants a new spirit within us so that we long to "walk in the Spirit, and not fulfill the lust of the flesh" (Galatians 5:16). We *want* the righteousness of the law to be fulfilled in us.

Our blessed assurance gives us two amazing gifts. First, we have the assurance of no condemnation. And second, we have the assurance of a new liberation. The Holy Spirit sets us free to please God with reckless abandon!

Did you notice that when you became a Christian, you found great joy in serving God? You experienced a deep joy in living for God and in pleasing Him. You *wanted* to do what God asked you to do. It's no longer a burden. That's what God does in salvation; He gives us His Spirit and enables us to walk in a way that pleases Him.

## JOINED TO THE SON

When you became a Christian, God the Father joined you to Jesus Christ, His Son. He did all of that through the work of the Holy Spirit.

"I am the vine," Jesus said, "you are the branches" (John 15:5). We are united to Christ! He accomplishes this miracle through the work of the Holy Spirit.

**Think of it:** God the Father, God the Son, and God the Holy Spirit all work together for your salvation! No wonder Paul could write, "Blessed be the God and Father of our Lord Jesus Christ, who has blessed us with every spiritual blessing in the heavenly places in Christ" (Ephesians 1:3).

O, what a Blessed Assurance it is to be found "in Christ"!

2

# A NEW LIBERATION

*For the law of the Spirit of life in Christ Jesus has made me free from the law of sin and death. For what the law could not do in that it was weak through the flesh, God did by sending His own Son in the likeness of sinful flesh, on account of sin: He condemned sin in the flesh, that the righteous requirement of the law might be fulfilled in us who do not walk according to the flesh but according to the Spirit.*

- *Romans 8:2-4*

The great American evangelist Billy Graham once said, "Man has two great spiritual needs: one is for forgiveness, and the other is for goodness."[3] Our hearts cry out to be forgiven and to be made righteous. Theologians use the terms "justified" and "sanctified."

In Christ, God provides both forgiveness and goodness. He saves us and liberates us. We no longer follow the dictates of our old, sinful nature; rather, we walk in the power and control of the Holy Spirit.

In other words, we have both forgiveness *and* goodness. What an amazing life the Lord wants to give us!

## WE HAVE A NEW LIBERATION

The first blessing of being in Christ, we've discovered, is that there is *no condemnation*. Notice that Paul now uses the same phrase "in Christ Jesus" in verse 2: "For the law of the Spirit of life in Christ Jesus has made me free from the law of sin and death."

The second blessing is that we have a *new liberation*. Paul tells us that those who are in Christ have been liberated. We have been freed in Jesus Christ. We have been liberated from the law of sin and death. In Jesus, sinners are forgiven and free.

Note that verses 2 and 3 both open with the word "for," while verse 4 opens with the word "that." Romans is a book of logic. In Romans 8, we find the connecting word "for" seventeen times. It signals Paul's rationale for what he's just said. Here in verse 2, because we're in Christ Jesus, "the Spirit of life in Christ Jesus has set us free."

What does "the law of the Spirit of life" mean? It refers to the Holy Spirit. Some say it's the gospel, but I believe it refers to the Holy Spirit.

And why does it say, "the law of the Spirit of life"? Paul uses the word "law" to convey the idea of a principle. He has in mind the life-giving law (or principle) of the Spirit.

When you become a Christian, everything changes because the Holy Spirit comes into your life. Someone without the Spirit, without God, without hope, doesn't have much going on. But when they receive new life, the Holy Spirit comes to live within them, radically changing their life. The Bible says, "Old things have passed away; behold, all things have become new" (2 Corinthians 5:17).

In Christ, you are a new creation. *Everything* changes when you become a Christian. You now have a life in the Spirit, the principle of the law of the life of the Spirit.

Only one God exists, the Bible says, but that one God exists in three persons. We refer to this as the Trinity. Although the word "Trinity" does not appear in the Bible, we use the term to describe God's triune nature. There is only one God, but that one God is manifested in three Persons: God the Father, God the Son, and God the Holy Spirit. Christians do not believe in three gods. Our God is one in essence (or nature) but exists as three separate Persons. Scripture refers to this as "the Godhead" (Romans 1:20; Colossians 2:9).

"I don't get it," you might be saying. Welcome to the club! Neither do I, even though I'm a preacher. No, I can't fully "explain" God.

God is transcendent, which means He is above us and beyond us. He's not like anything we can know, touch, see, smell, feel, or sense. As finite beings, we cannot explain the exact nature of our infinite God. We can, though, worship "God in three Persons, blessed Trinity," as the old hymn says. He is One, in essence, three in persons.

The Spirit indwells you, He fills you, and He seals you "unto the day of redemption" (Ephesians 4:30). He is the Comforter, the *Parakletos* (John 14:16). He comes alongside you to comfort you and strengthen you. We're about to learn that you cannot live the Christian life apart from the Holy Spirit. He's the One who makes you a Christian, enables and strengthens you to live the Christian life.

## SET FREE FROM WHAT?

We move from justification in Romans 8:1 to sanctification in verses 2-4, moving from forgiveness to goodness to holy living in the Christian walk. Paul tells us we've been set free by the work of the Holy Spirit. Someone once said, "Jesus died for us so the Spirit could live in us."

Set free from what? We've been liberated "from the law of sin and death." The Holy Spirit, "the Spirit of life in Christ Jesus," has "made me free from the law of sin and death."

And what is "the law of sin and death"? It is a sin principle of our sinful nature. It is indwelling sin. Some say, alternatively, it's God's written law because it brings about sin and death in our lives. That's also possible.

The law doesn't *make* me sin; it just reveals that I'm a sinner. As a result, it brings about sin and death in a lesser sense. Someone once said, "God's law is the occasion of both sin and death." Paul said, "I would not have known sin except through the law. For I would not have known covetousness unless the law had said, "You shall not covet" (Romans 7:7).

I think Paul has more in mind here than the law of God. He's talking about a principle of the sin nature. Even as a Christian, you still have the capacity and ability to sin. But the law of the Spirit of life has set you free from that indwelling sin nature.

At the end of Romans 7, Paul cried out, "O wretched man that I am! Who will deliver me from this body of death?" Then he answered, "I thank God," it's been done "through Jesus Christ our Lord! So then, with the mind I myself serve the law of God, but with the flesh the law of sin." He was saying, "I want to do what's right, but I'm in this battle."

When we arrive at Romans 8, we find out that liberty, deliverance, and freedom all come from life in the Spirit. It's the law of the Spirit.

Think of the law of gravity. If I were to drop my Bible, it would fall. If I hold up the same Bible, I supersede the law of gravity. We deal with this law of sin and death in a similar way. Sin wants to pull me down, but the Holy Spirit comes to lift me up, give me strength, and empower me to soar over the law of sin and death. A poet once wrote,

> "Do this and live!" the law commands,
>
> But gives me neither feet nor hands.
>
> But sweeter sounds the Gospel brings,
>
> It bids me fly and gives me wings!

I can override the law of sin and death with the law of the life of the Spirit. There really is victory for those in Christ Jesus. We can walk in new liberty.

## BUT, HOW?

How does God bring us this new liberty? How do we come into it? Notice the how in verse 3: "For what the law could not do in that it was weak through the flesh...."

God did something that neither the law nor we could do. God did this "by sending His own Son in the likeness of sinful flesh, on account of sin: He condemned sin in the flesh" (verse 3).

Notice that verse 3 starts again with a "for," giving us the apostle's rationale. Paul first tells us what it's not: It doesn't happen by the law. You can't live the Christian life by the law or by legalism. Paul says, "For what the law *could not* do...." The law could not bring forgiveness or goodness. It can't deliver you or set you free.

Why can't the law do this? Paul answers that "it was weak through the flesh." The problem is not the law. The law could not set you free "in that it was weak through the flesh." God's law is holy, just, and good, but it has the power only to show you your sin and condemn you for your disobedience. It cannot bring forgiveness, and it doesn't bring goodness. But what the law could not do, God has done by providing His own dear Son.

So then, how exactly are we set free? *God* sets us free.

When all hope is gone, and we're condemned, God steps in. God takes the initiative. He does what the law could never do. The Bible says that we love Him because "He first loved us" (1 John 4:19). If it weren't for God in His mercy and grace, seeing us in our sinful plight and taking the initiative to reach out to us, we would remain lost.

## TWO DIVINE ACTS OF LIBERATION

Paul describes two things God has done to set us free.

First, *God sent His own Son.* That's the Christmas message. That's the gospel. That's what God did. We love Him because He first loved us and sent His Son. God the Father sent God the Son so that we could be forgiven. God, in His love, sent Jesus, who died on the Cross, so that we could have the forgiveness of our sins, no condemnation, and the Holy Spirit. Because of Christ's death on Calvary and because of Pentecost, we have both forgiveness and goodness.

John 3:16 carries a similar message: "For God so loved the world that He gave His only begotten Son." God sent His own Son, His only unique Son. There was no other. There is no one like Jesus. No other has ever been virgin born, like Jesus. No other has ever lived a sinless life like Jesus. No other died a substitutionary death on the Cross for the sins of the world like Jesus. No one ever rose from the dead like Jesus. No one ever ascended back to heaven like Jesus. No one ever was seated at the right hand of the Father like Jesus. And no one but Jesus—praise God! —will come again to establish His kingdom forever and ever.

We have hope in Jesus Christ. God sent His only Son, in love, to save us.

Second, God sent His only Son "in the likeness of sinful flesh." Here we see the Incarnation when God the Son became flesh or took on humanity. That happened through the virgin birth, which led to Christ's sinless life. All of these are implied in the statement, "in the likeness of sinful flesh."

Had Paul said, "in sinful flesh," that would mean that Jesus was not virgin born and was, therefore, a sinner, so His death on the Cross could not have atoned for anyone's sin but His own. But Jesus was both human and God. His humanity didn't lessen His deity, nor did His deity lessen His humanity. He was the God-man—one person, two natures; divine and human.

God did what we could not do. He sent His Son through the womb of the Virgin Mary. As the God-man, Jesus lived a sinless life, making it possible for Him to die for our sins.

## BUT, WHY?

Why did God send His Son? He did so "on account of sin."

This phrase conveys the idea of the atonement or the Cross. More literally, it's "concerning sin" or "as a sin offering." Why did God, in His love, send His Son—sinless and with full humanity—to die a substitutionary death on the Cross? The answer is "on account of sin."

Do you remember when the angel Gabriel came to Joseph to assure him that Mary's pregnancy was the work of the Holy Spirit? Gabriel told Joseph that he would have a son and said, "You shall call His name JESUS, for He will save His people from their sins" (Matthew 1:21). That's what Jesus came to do: to save us from our sins. The name "Jesus" literally means "God is salvation." It's the New Testament equivalent of the Old Testament, "Yeshua" or "Jehovah saves." The name "Jesus" means "God saves," and that's why He came.

But note a second reason why God sent His Son: "He condemned sin in the flesh." God sent His Son "on account of sin" to atone for sin (that's the Incarnation and Crucifixion), but He also sent His Son to "condemn sin in the flesh" (that's goodness). Here we have, again, both forgiveness and goodness.

The sinless life of Jesus Christ is given to us or imputed to us so that we can walk in newness of life. God saves us not just to take us to heaven someday but to make us holy while we continue to live on the earth.

What does it mean that God condemned "sin in the flesh"? Jesus took upon Himself, that is, upon His own flesh, all our sins. Peter explains that Jesus "Himself bore our sins in His own body on the tree, that we, having died to sins, might live for righteousness—by whose stripes you were healed" (1 Peter 2:24). On the Cross, God condemned our sin so that we could be set free from sin's penalty, power, and one day, its very presence altogether.

And it gets even better! Paul clarifies the reason why God sent His own Son to condemn our sin in Him. He did so to *make us holy*. He sent His own Son to the Cross "that the righteous requirement of the law might be fulfilled in us who do not walk according to the flesh but according to the Spirit" (v. 4). God saves us to make us holy.

In both Testaments, God said, "Be holy, for I am holy" (Leviticus 11:44-45; 1 Peter 1:16). If you're a child of God, then you should be like your Father in heaven. If God is holy, then you should be holy. As we've seen, the ideas of "saint," "sanctified," and "holy" all come from the same root word in Greek (*hagios*), which means "to be set apart, made holy."

Justification is our position—we're declared righteous. Justification is God declaring us positionally righteous, with no progression or degree. All of us are equally righteous before God.

Sanctification is our practice—we're made righteous through the ongoing work of the Spirit. In sanctification, God comes to live inside us and makes us holy.

Someone put it like this: "Justification is me in Christ; sanctification is Christ in me." Not only am I in Christ, but Christ is in me through the work of the Holy Spirit to make me righteous. This is all about living a holy life.

## THREE IMPORTANT OBSERVATIONS

Let me make three important statements and observations.

1. Holy living is salvation's goal.

Holy living is the goal of your salvation. God didn't save you just so you can go to heaven someday. God saved you so that *right now*, you'll live a holy life. You're a saint positionally, but you need to be a saint practically.

People sometimes say, "Pastor John, I don't know what God's will is for me." I can truthfully respond, "I know God's will for you. I can tell *everyone* what God's will is for them, because it's the same for everyone: 'Be holy, for I am holy.'"

God's will is that you cooperate with His Spirit to make you more like Jesus Christ. The goal of sanctification is Christlikeness.

Most of us are familiar with Ephesians 2:8-9, which says, "For by grace you have been saved through faith, and that not of yourselves; it is the gift of God, not of works, lest anyone should boast." We are probably less familiar with verse 10, where Paul adds, "For we are His workmanship, created in Christ Jesus for good works, which God prepared beforehand that we should walk in them."

What does it mean to be "God's workmanship"? It's an amazing word in Greek (*poiema*). It means "something created, or something made," like a work of art. We get the English word "poem" from it. You and I are God's *poiema*, God's work of art.

Some of us have a long way to go!

Have you ever seen an artist paint a picture? When he starts putting the first brush strokes on it, you think, *This dude is a lousy painter! That looks terrible!* But then, as he begins to bring it all together and adds the background, you say, "Wow! That artist clearly knew what he was doing!" At first, it looked like the guy needed a lot of help and had no talent, but now it becomes *very* clear that he is a gifted artist.

*You* are God's work of art, so be patient. Maybe every Christian should have a sign around their neck saying, "Be patient; under construction," or "Forgive the mess; work ongoing." God isn't finished with us yet.

Of course, some people have progressed a lot more than others in the construction process. God has chipped away a lot of the pieces that don't look like Jesus so that only the things that look like Jesus remain. One of the primary ways God uses to sanctify you and make you more like Jesus is through suffering.

"Oh, I don't like that!" someone says. "Let's change the subject."

None of us wants pain and discomfort. We don't want difficulty. But how is God going to make you patient if you never have to be patient? How is God going to make you forgiving if you never have to forgive anyone? How is God going to teach you to love if you have nobody unlovely to love?

"I love only lovely people," someone replies. That means you love very few people.

We need to value character over comfort. I'm lecturing my own heart right now because I have the gift of gripe. I'm gifted at complaining; it just flows from me. But if I realize that God is trying to make me more like Jesus, and if I value character over comfort, my trials will not upset me. Do you know why your trials upset you so much? Because you want comfort over character.

God is working in you; you're under construction. He's in the process of trying to make you more holy.

We love to talk about the forgiveness of God, but what about the holiness of God? God wants to make you and me more like Jesus Christ. He allows suffering, trials, and difficulties in our lives to conform us to the image of His Son. He uses His Spirit, His Word, prayer, and other spiritual disciplines to shape us, mold us, and make us more closely into the image of His Son, Jesus Christ. And He does all this so that He can condemn sin in the flesh.

Holy living is salvation's goal.

2. Holy living consists of fulfilling the law's just demands.

God wants His righteous demands, as seen in the law, to be fulfilled in us. The Word says "in" us, not "by" us. When God works in us, by His Spirit, His work manifests itself in our lives as we obey Him. The righteousness of the law can be fulfilled in us!

This is what's called "The New Covenant," described in Jeremiah 31:33, where God said, "I will put My law in their minds and write it on their hearts."

I grew up in church and knew the Bible my whole life, but not until I was born again did I want to read the Bible, love the Bible, or love God—and oh, I wanted to! Today, I want to walk with God, serve God, and follow God because the Spirit came inside me and gave me that strength and ability. He wrote His laws upon my heart.

3. Holy living is the work of the Holy Spirit.

Verse 4 describes believers "who do not walk according to the flesh [that's your sinful nature] but according to the Spirit." The Christian life is a life in and a walk by the power of the Holy Spirit. You cannot live the Christian life without the Holy Spirit. God the Father sent God the Son so that we could have God the Holy Spirit dwelling inside us.

And *how* do we walk in the Spirit? Ephesians 5:18 answers, "Do not be drunk with wine, in which is dissipation [or "debauchery"]; but be filled with the Spirit." He gives us a negative and then a positive. First, don't be intoxicated by alcohol. Second, do be filled with or controlled by the Spirit. In the original Greek, that statement is a command, an imperative. It's not an option. God commands every Christian to be Spirit-filled.

Someone says, "I thought all Christians had the Holy Spirit."

They do, but the Holy Spirit doesn't have all Christians. Again, the question is not, "Do you have the Holy Spirit?" but rather, "Does the Holy Spirit have you?"

Being filled with the Holy Spirit means that He controls you, but not as if you're a robot. He controls your thoughts; they're holy. He controls your words; they're holy. He controls your attitudes; they're holy. He controls your actions; they're holy. Just as you do stupid things when you're under the influence of alcohol, now you do holy things when you're under the influence of the Holy Spirit.

When the Holy Spirit directs your life, He brings His fruit into your life: His love, His joy, His peace, His goodness, His mercy, His kindness, and His self-control. The greatest evidence of the Spirit-filled life is fruit. God doesn't want religious nuts; He wants spiritual fruit. He wants love, joy, peace, gentleness, meekness, self-control, temperance, and faithfulness to blossom in your life through the work of the Spirit.

And *how* are we filled with the fruit of the Spirit? Put Ephesians 5:18 right alongside Colossians 3:16, where Paul says, "Let the Word of Christ dwell in you richly." To be Spirit-filled brings the same results as being Word-filled. You cannot be a Spirit-filled Christian if you neglect the Bible.

People regularly say to me, "Pastor, I don't know what's wrong; my Christian life is so weak. I just keep falling into sin."

I ask them, "Are you reading your Bible?"

"No, I don't have time. I'm too busy sinning."

The Bible will keep you from sin, or sin will keep you from the Bible. The psalmist said, "Your Word I have hidden in my heart, that I might not sin against You" (Psalm 119:11). Scripture is "a lamp to my feet and a light to my path" (Psalm 119:105).

Why do pastors like me teach the Bible as we do on Sunday mornings? Certainly not because it's fashionable. We teach it because this is the way to holiness. When you grow in the knowledge of God's Word, you'll grow in grace, you'll learn to lean on the Spirit, you'll become more like Christ...and God will change your life. The Spirit of God takes the Word of God and transforms the child of God into the image of Jesus Christ, the Son of God.

God sent His Son to die for us—that's forgiveness—and He sent His Spirit to live in us—that's goodness.

## A FAVORITE STORY

John 8 tells one of my favorite Bible stories. Certain religious leaders brought to Jesus a woman who was caught in the very act of adultery. They threw her down and said, "Jesus, Moses, in the law, commanded us to stone this woman. But what do *You* say?"

Jesus bent down and started doodling in the dirt, a common practice in those days. They didn't have computers, phones, or pencils and paper, so they smoothed out the dirt and wrote on it. One of the first things I will ask Jesus when I get to heaven is, "What did You write in the dirt that day?" John didn't tell us, and not knowing drives me crazy.

As Jesus continued to write in the dirt, they pressed Him: "The law commands that she should be stoned. What do You say?" Jesus straightened up and replied, "Let him who is without sin cast the first stone."

Some theorize that Jesus might have been writing the Ten Commandments next to the names of the woman's accusers. "Thou shalt not commit adultery—Rabbi Shammai." The rabbi saw his name next to the commandment and blurted out, "You know, I have a dental appointment right now. I gotta go," and he took off. Maybe. The Bible doesn't say. But it does say that from the oldest to the youngest, every accuser wanted out of there. Could that be because the oldest had the most sins? Who knows? But whatever Jesus wrote, they all started to slither away, leaving Jesus standing there alone with this woman.

"Where are your accusers?" Jesus asked her. "Has no one condemned you?"

"No one, Lord," she replied.

"Then neither do I condemn you," Jesus said. "Go and sin no more."

At that moment, Jesus gave the woman both forgiveness and goodness. "I don't condemn you. Now go and live a life of holiness."

And that, friends, is the Christian life.

# 3

# LIFE IN THE SPIRIT

*For they that are after the flesh do mind the things of the flesh; but they that are after the Spirit the things of the Spirit. For to be carnally minded is death; but to be spiritually minded is life and peace. Because the carnal mind is enmity against God: for it is not subject to the law of God, neither indeed can be. So then they that are in the flesh cannot please God. But ye are not in the flesh, but in the Spirit, if so be that the Spirit of God dwell in you. Now if any man have not the Spirit of Christ, he is none of his. And if Christ be in you, the body is dead because of sin; but the Spirit is life because of righteousness. But if the Spirit of him that raised up Jesus from the dead dwell in you, he that raised up Christ from the dead shall also quicken your mortal bodies by his Spirit that dwelleth in you. Therefore, brethren, we are debtors, not to the flesh, to live after the flesh. For if ye live after the flesh, ye shall die: but if ye through the Spirit do mortify the deeds of the body, ye shall live.*

*- Romans 8:5-13 KJV*

To be a Christian is to have a new life in the Spirit. Before your conversion, you were in the flesh; after conversion, you are in the Spirit. Before you were a Christian, you had only one life and one walk, and that was in the flesh—the sinful, carnal nature.

In Romans 8:5-13, we see a great contrast between these two ways of living. You can live after the flesh or you can live after the Spirit. The Spirit fills and empowers believers to enable us to walk in a way that pleases God.

## TWO WAYS TO LIVE

Paul tells us that the Holy Spirit wants to do two primary things in our lives. First, He wants our minds under His control (verses 5-8). Second, He wants us to mortify the members or our bodies (verses 9-13). In other words, He wants us to crucify the flesh and to walk in the Spirit.

Let's look first at the fact that *the Holy Spirit wants to control our minds.* In verse 5, Paul contrasts two mindsets. "For those who live according to the flesh set their minds on the things of the flesh, but those who live according to the Spirit, the things of the Spirit." He implies that one kind of individual follows the dictates of the flesh while the other follows the things of the Spirit.

The key question here is, who are those who live according to the flesh? I think it is best to understand them as non-Christians.

It is possible for a Christian to be in the flesh or to lapse into the flesh. You can be born again and still live carnally. You'll find that out if you drive the freeways of Southern California! It really is possible for a Christian to be in the flesh.

But the flesh does not have to dictate and control what you do; if the Spirit lives within you, you no longer have to be dominated by the flesh in your mind, outlook, or attitude. As a Christian, your orientation or inclination—the bent of your life, the tenor of your life—is spiritual rather than carnal. The old, sinful, Adamic nature does not have to control you as it did before Jesus saved you.

One of my goals in teaching is to convey the actual meaning of the text, not to impose on it what I want it to say. It would be easy to focus on carnal Christianity here, but that's not what Paul is talking about. He's talking about non-Christians, "those who are in the flesh," the unsaved, unbelievers, those who haven't been born again.

Notice it says that they are "after the flesh." The word "flesh" here means their sinful nature. When Adam sinned in the Garden of Eden, he brought sin and death to the whole human race. He acted as a federal head and brought sin and death to us all. Every human being is born with an Adamic, sinful bent. That's what Paul means by "flesh." He's not talking about our physical bodies but about our sinful capacity or our sin nature.

These people mind "the things of the flesh." They have a carnal mind. They think only about physical, sinful things. The carnal man cannot understand the things of the Spirit. Paul says that is so because the things of the Spirit are "spiritually discerned" (1 Corinthians 2:14). A non-Christian does not understand the Bible, the Holy Spirit, heaven, hell, or the things of God. He doesn't understand the things that have eternal value. He is temporal-minded, absorbed in the mundane and the physical.

Jesus described the carnal man in Matthew 6, where He tells us not to worry because we are God's children. Worry, He said, is something that non-Christians do. They worry about what they're going to eat, what they're going to drink, and what they're going to wear.

People come to church and don't even hear the sermon because they're thinking, *Where will we go to lunch after church? What are we going to wear? Where are we going to go shopping? Who's going to mow the lawn? How am*

*I going to pay the bills?* The natural man is consumed with and worried about these things.

If you are a child of God, your Father in heaven knows that you need these things. He'll take care of you. "Seek first the kingdom of God and His righteousness, and all these things shall be added to you" (Matthew 6:33). He'll take care of what you eat and drink and the clothes that you wear.

John describes the natural man, the unbeliever, the man or woman in the flesh, when he warns us, "Do not love the world or the things in the world." The word translated "world" is the Greek term *cosmos*, which speaks of the evil world system apart from God. Then John breaks it down into the "lust of the flesh, the lust of the eyes and the pride of life" (1 John 2:15-16).

Think of the lust of the flesh as your passions. The unbeliever is governed and controlled by his passions, his bodily appetites. The lust of the eyes refers to your possessions: "Oh if I could only have more things! If I could just have a bigger house (or more houses), a new car, or nicer clothes." We somehow think that life consists of the abundance of things we possess. It doesn't. The pride of life refers to your position or status: "Look what I've accomplished! I'm a self-made man." Such a man worships himself and feels smug about who he is.

You can be a moral person, not wicked by the world's standards, and still be in the flesh. Your flesh, your bodily appetites, and the things of this world dominate you. Maybe you go to church; maybe you're religious. In fact, the worst kind of "in the flesh" people are religious. They take pride in their robes, rites, rituals, and religion: "Look who I am! Look what I've done!" They think they're wonderful because they've been confirmed or baptized, take communion, or have a particular religious persuasion.

The passage we're about to investigate declares plainly that those who are in the flesh cannot please God. If you're not a Christian, nothing you do brings pleasure to God. None of your accomplishments earns you merit or favor with God.

Verse 6 declares another characteristic of unsaved people: “To be carnally minded is death.” They are dead in their sins and separated from God. When they read the Bible, they don’t see it as any big deal. When you’re not born again, you think, *Whatever. I’m not into the Bible. Going to church bores me. I don’t like the songs they sing. Worship and pray? I don’t want to do that*. Why not? Because they’re dead spiritually. They have no spiritual life.

Verse 7 tells us that the carnal mind, the fleshly mind, is at war with God. If you’re not a Christian, you’re an enemy of God, whether you realize it or not. God is not at war with you, but you are at war with God. Such a person has no peace.

When Paul repeats the word “mind” or “minded,” he’s talking about our attitude, outlook, and focus on life. He’s talking about our inner personality, who we are inside—our mind, emotions, will—the real us.

The real you is not your physical body. The real you expresses who you are. You are an immaterial person inside a material body. If you’re a Christian, you leave your body and go to heaven when you die. In nonbelievers, the mind, the outlook, and the attitudes live according to the dictates of the flesh.

Paul insists, “The carnal mind . . . is not subject to the law of God.” Carnally minded people are at war with God, which means they’re not subject to the law of God. Paul says, “nor indeed can be.” In verse 8, he says, “Those who are in the flesh [unbelievers] cannot please God.” Don’t forget that. It’s important.

“Well,” you say, “maybe they’re a good person.”

They “cannot please God.”

"Well, maybe they've been baptized."

They "cannot please God."

Years ago, a man in my church sat under my preaching for some time. He shocked me one day after a big accident occurred on the freeway near our church. When a large motorhome caught fire, a good Samaritan pulled up behind it, got out of his car, ran into the motorhome, and pulled the family to safety, just in time to save them from certain death. Then the motorhome blew up.

This parishioner said, "Pastor John, because of the good thing that guy did, certainly *he's* going to go to heaven—isn't he?"

I thought, *Where have you been*? Someone must run into a burning motorhome and save people so that God will let them into heaven? I don't think so.

The Bible says we can do *nothing* to earn, merit, or deserve heaven. Some people think that if you give your life for your nation in war, certainly God will let you into heaven. But is that what the Bible says? Listen carefully: "Those who are in the flesh CANNOT please God."

Regardless of who you are or what you've done, your best before a holy God is like filthy rags. The Bible says, "There is none righteous. No, not one" (Psalm 14:1-3).

Maybe you go to church. Maybe you say, "I'm going to endure this guy's sermon. If I do it every week, then God will let me into heaven because I've suffered so much on earth." When you stand before God and say, "You'd better let me in heaven! I listened to that pastor's awful sermons for *six years*! Every Sunday! Anyone who endures that kind of agony deserves to go to heaven!" You won't be let in. The only thing that will get you inside is if you reach out by faith and take the hand of Jesus Christ, who died on the Cross for you, was buried, and rose from the dead.

Please, be crystal clear about this: *unsaved people cannot please God.* Only true Christians can please God.

## THE HOLY SPIRIT WANTS TO CONTROL OUR MINDS

Let's look at the contrast in verse 5: "but those who live according to the Spirit [or "the orientation of the Spirit," "the inclination of the Spirit," or "the direction of the Spirit"] set their minds on the things of the Spirit." These are Christians. Paul is talking about people who have been born again into God's family.

The man of the flesh "minds the things of the flesh," but those who live according to the Spirit "mind the things of the Spirit." Believers set their minds, focus their attention, and fasten the tenor of their life on "the things of the Spirit."

Paul writes elsewhere, "If then you were raised with Christ, seek those things which are above," or "set your mind or affections on things above" (Colossians 3:1-3). Christians should set their minds on things above and not on things of the earth. Why? "You are dead, and your life is hidden with Christ in God."

Some say, "You Christians are so heavenly minded that you're of no earthly good." That's hardly the problem in the church today. The problem is that Christians are too earthly-minded to be of any good to heaven. I pray to God that we become more heavenly-minded!

Being spiritually minded doesn't mean that you put on a white robe and stand on a mountain waiting for the Rapture. It doesn't mean you sit all day and pray, talk to God, fast, and become a holy man.

The work of the Holy Spirit in the life of the believer has one goal in mind: to glorify Jesus Christ. That's all. He wants to make believers more like Jesus so that Jesus gets the glory. That's why the Holy Spirit has come, not to glorify us but to glorify Jesus.

Paul used the same word "mind" in Philippians 2, where he said, "Let this mind [this attitude, this outlook] be in you which was also in Christ Jesus, who, being in the form of God, did not consider it robbery to be equal with God." Jesus did not try to hold onto or cling to the glory that was rightly His as the Son of God, but He "emptied Himself and took on the form of a servant and became obedient to the point of death, even the death of the cross." Jesus, who is God, humbled Himself and took on humanity. He became a servant and delighted to obey the Father's will, even though that will took Him to the Cross.

When the Spirit works in our lives, not only does He glorify Jesus, but He makes us like Jesus and gives us a servant's heart so that we put others first. As a result, we consider others more important than ourselves.

## MARKS OF THE SPIRIT-FILLED BELIEVER

Several qualities characterize the life of a Spirit-filled believer.

- Those who mind the things of the Spirit have a real appetite for the Bible.

I'll never forget when I first got saved. I was nineteen years old, just out of high school, and even though I was raised in Sunday school and church, I was a prodigal. I had fallen away. I got a little wild for a few years, then got out of high school. God convicted me, and I got saved.

For the first time in my life, I started reading the Bible, although I was almost illiterate. I'd bluffed my way through high school. I almost couldn't read. I came up short in credits, and they kicked me out of school; they didn't want me around anymore. When I got saved after high school, I learned to read by reading the Bible. And I couldn't get enough of it.

I was living with my parents at the time. One day, I was at home, in my bedroom, reading the Bible. When my mom opened the door and saw me, she nearly died and went to heaven. She just started praising the Lord: "I thank You, Jesus! There is a God in heaven!"

And then I started to pray. I freaked *myself* out. I pinched myself. "This is me?" I'm reading my Bible . . . and *liking* it. I'm praying and talking to God . . . and hearing His voice. *This is amazing!*

And then, I went to church, which blew my parents' minds. I had long hair and a big beard. They took me back to our little Pentecostal church with about sixty people. Everyone there was over eighty years old. When I showed up, they freaked out. They thought Jesus had returned.

"Wow! Praise God! Hippie John got saved and came to church!" Then they sang and worshipped God . . . *and I liked it.* We hugged. What a blessing! It was *amazing*!

*What's happened to me?* I wondered.

What happened to me is that I got saved. I was born again. The Bible says of saved people, "Old things have passed away, behold, all things have become new" (2 Corinthians 5:17). The things I used to hate I now love, and the things I used to love I now hate.

Verse 6 says that those who are in the Spirit or "spiritually minded" enjoy both "life and peace." If you haven't been born again, you don't know what you're missing. You don't have life: "For God so loved the world that He gave His only begotten Son, that whosoever believeth in Him shall not perish but have everlasting life" (John 3:16).

Everlasting life is life in a new sphere. It's life with a new quality. It's not just living in heaven forever; it's life *right now*, but with a new quality. It's life in a new dimension. It's a spiritual life.

Before you were a Christian, you were in the flesh, dead in your sins, and separated from God. Now you have the life of God in your soul. I think that's the best definition of a Christian: one who has the life of God in their soul.

A Christian also has peace. That's peace *with* God—the war is over—and now you also have the peace *of* God. Marriage is difficult if you're not a Christian because all you know is the flesh and the dictates of the flesh. When someone comes to me with marriage problems, the first thing I want to know is whether they know Jesus. Have they been born again? Have they trusted Jesus Christ as their Lord and Savior? I can't do much to help them unless they first give their heart to Jesus Christ.

When you know Jesus, your marriage involves three persons: you, your spouse, and Jesus. And the Bible says that "a threefold cord is not easily broken" (Ecclesiastes 4:12). It's no longer just a husband and a wife; it's Jesus in the middle of that relationship as the foundation of that relationship.

This doesn't mean that Christians have no problems in marriage! We, too, can yield to the flesh. But when the Lord is in your heart, you have the Holy Spirit in you to be able to love one another and serve one another. You want God's glory. You want Jesus to be glorified in that relationship. And you have the capacity to obey God's law.

Verse 8 says, "Those who are in the flesh cannot please God." It implies that those who *are* in the Spirit *can* please God. Verse 8 gives us only the negative, but we can infer that if we're in the Spirit, we can please God by the way we live.

Our minds matter.

## THE WORK OF THE SPIRIT

The Holy Spirit is mentioned ten times in verses 5 to 13. The Spirit wants to control your mind, your attitude, and your outlook. Paul tells us in Romans 12:1-2, "I beseech you . . . by the mercies of God, that you present your bodies a living sacrifice, holy, acceptable to God, which is your reasonable service. And do not be conformed to this world [the Phillips translation says, 'don't let the world press you into its mold'] but be transformed by the renewing of your mind."

We renew our minds through the Word of God and prayer. Do you want to walk in the Spirit as a believer? If so, then spend time in God's Word and spend time in prayer. It will transform your life.

We find a second main division in verses 9-13, where Paul says that we, through the Spirit, should mortify our members. He wants us to take a step of faith, present our bodies to Him, and realize our old life is dead. We need to crucify the flesh with its affections and lusts.

Verse 9 tells us that a Christian is someone in whom the Holy Spirit dwells. "But you [Paul contrasts people of the flesh with the man or woman of the Spirit] are not in the flesh but in the Spirit, if indeed the Spirit of God dwells in you. Now if anyone does not have the Spirit of Christ [another name for the Holy Spirit] he is not His." Paul makes it very clear that if you do not have the Holy Spirit, you are not a Christian. You don't belong to God. You are not a child of God.

Don't ever let someone tell you that you can be a Christian and not have the Spirit. *All* Christians have the Holy Spirit, but not all Christians are under the control of the Spirit. Again, it's not whether you have the Spirit but whether the Spirit has you. The question is not whether you have the Holy Spirit inside you; that's true of all Christians. But does the Holy Spirit control you and empower you?

When I meet someone who says, "I'm a Christian, but I don't read the Bible," I think, *How can you be a Christian and not want to read the Bible? It's your spiritual food! It's how you hear God speak. It's how you grow.*

God uses His Word to sanctify us. When Jesus prayed His great high-priestly prayer in John 17, He said, "Sanctify them by Your truth. Your word is truth" (verse 17). To be Spirit-filled, you must be Word-filled. The Bible and the Word of God must work together to make you like the Son of God.

Spirit-filled Christians also want fellowship. It's a contradiction in terms to say, "I'm a Christian, but I don't go to church." When I got saved, I didn't care if the church people were old, didn't look like me, or weren't into what I was into. We were all into Jesus and were brothers and sisters in Christ. I found sweet communion and sweet fellowship there.

Some say, "I don't go to church because there are too many hypocrites there."

"Well," I say, "we can always use another one. Come join us."

"I went to church once and found some weird people there."

"And where aren't there weird people?"

"Sorry, but I'm looking for the perfect church."

"If you do find it," I might say, "don't join it, because you'll ruin it. It won't be perfect anymore."

We sinners who are saved by grace come together for fellowship. We're forgiven by the blood of Jesus Christ. We stumble and fall, but the tenor of our lives is to walk in the Spirit and to glorify God.

We also like to pray. We want to sing. I love that Paul says, "Be filled with the Spirit, speaking to one another in psalms and hymns and spiritual songs, singing and making melody in your heart to the Lord" (Ephesians 5:18-19). I don't understand how someone says, "I'm a Christian, but I'm not one of the singing kind. It makes me uncomfortable."

"Then you probably don't want to go to heaven," I might say, "because we'll be doing a lot of that up there."

The original Greek text behind our translation, "singing and making melody in your heart to the Lord," really means the Holy Spirit plucks strings in our hearts. The term is used for a stringed instrument. One indication that you are a Christian is that you have a song in your heart. It may not be a great song, but it's a song. So, the Bible says, "Make a joyful noise unto the Lord" (Psalm 95:2).

The Spirit even gives us songs in the night. Remember how Luke describes the time when Paul and Silas were beaten and put in prison (Acts 16)? At midnight, they began to sing praises to God, and their fellow prisoners heard them.

When you lie in bed at night, God puts a song in your heart. When you get up in the morning, God puts a song in your heart. Throughout the day, God puts a song in your heart.

When I got saved, I went everywhere with two things: my Bible and a hymnal. A. W. Tozer said those are the two most important books to the Christian. I remember when I took my lunch breaks. I went outside, opened my Bible, read, and then I opened a hymnal and sang. I'll never forget the first time I came upon the song *Amazing Grace* as a young Christian. Even though I had heard it all my life, I'd never sung it as a Christian, and one stanza stunned me:

> When we've been there ten thousand years,
>
> Bright shining as the sun,
>
> We've no less days to sing God's praise
>
> Than when we first begun.
>
> – John Newton, "Amazing Grace! (how sweet the sound)"

I began to weep like a baby because of the reality of heaven. I'm going to heaven! God has saved me! I knew I could still have been living in darkness. All my friends were going to prison for doing drugs, but God had reached out and saved me by His grace.

I love the Word, and I love to sing. I love to pray, and I love to go to church. All of this makes me think, God, how good You are!

Another mark of true, Spirit-filled, indwelt believers is that they love Jesus and seek to glorify Him. In verse 9, Paul calls the Holy Spirit "the Spirit of Christ." The Spirit comes to glorify Jesus Christ. He gives you a love for Jesus Christ and a longing to spend time with Him.

## TWO CONSEQUENCES OF THE SPIRIT'S INDWELLING

After affirming the Spirit as the distinguishing mark of a Christian, Paul gives two consequences of the Holy Spirit's indwelling.

Verse 10 opens with "And if," while verse 11 opens with "But if." Both signal two consequences of the Holy Spirit's indwelling. Paul writes, "And if Christ is in you [or, 'since Christ is in you'] the body is dead because of sin, but the Spirit is life because of righteousness" (v. 10).

Paul said the same thing in a different way in another passage, where he wrote that the "outward man is perishing, yet the inward man is being renewed day by day" (2 Corinthians 4:16). The older you get, the more your body weakens and begins to perish. If you don't believe me, look at your high school annuals—and weep: "That was me; I actually had hair!" You look at those photos and say, "Wow! What happened?"

It's simple: The outward man is perishing.

But the inward man grows stronger and is being renewed day by day. You have a future and a hope as a believer! The body dies, but the Spirit brings life.

About the second consequence, Paul says in verse 11, "But if the Spirit of Him who raised Jesus from the dead dwells in you, He [the Holy Spirit] who raised Christ from the dead will also give life to your mortal bodies through His Spirit who dwells in you." Paul implies there that the Holy Spirit raised Christ from the dead. In various places, Scripture says that the Father raised Jesus from the dead, that Jesus raised Himself, and that the Holy Spirit raised Jesus. All three Persons of the Trinity—the Father, the Son, and the Holy Spirit—raised Christ from the dead.

Paul says that because you have the Holy Spirit in your body, which is dead because of sin, one day it will be resurrected. The same Holy Spirit who raised Jesus from the dead will one day raise *your* body from the dead. This will happen either when you're raptured or when Christ comes back to earth. At that time, "the dead in Christ will rise first" (1 Thessalonians 4:16). But whether you die before the Rapture and your body gets buried or cremated or thrown into the sea, or you're alive at the Rapture, one day your body *will* be metamorphosized and changed "in a moment, in the twinkling of an eye" (1 Corinthians 15:52). Your body will be reunited with your soul and spirit. You will have a brand new, glorified body in heaven—new and improved.

In one sermon, I spoke like this quite excitedly, and after the service, a grandmother and her grandson came down the aisle to say hello. This little boy, maybe eight or nine years old, had a big smile on his face. He was missing his right leg from his knee down and walked on a blade. His whole face glowed.

"My grandson and I were in the loft listening to the sermon," she told me, "and when you said, 'We're going to get a new body,' he turned to me and just smiled and beamed real big. He wanted to come to say thank you for your sermon.'"

I hugged him, and we talked. "You're going to have two legs," I told him, "and you're going to run and leap and walk in heaven." What an awesome reality that someday we're going to have new bodies!

Where can you get hope like that outside of Christ? The world doesn't offer it. The flesh can't give it. But when you come to know Christ, you have that assurance. Even now, the Holy Spirit works day by day to renew our bodies.

## LIVE AFTER THE SPIRIT!

Paul starts closing his thoughts in verses 12-13 with the word "therefore." He says, "Therefore, brethren [speaking of the believers], we are debtors, not to the flesh [we owe the old, sinful life nothing], to live according to the flesh. For if you live according to the flesh you will die; but if by the Spirit you put to death the deeds of the body you will live."

The Bible tells us to "mortify" or "put to death" the deeds of the body. How do we accomplish that? The Bible says we do this "by the Spirit" (v. 13). We cannot live the victorious Christian life without the Holy Spirit.

Jesus said, "If your right eye offends you"—that is, if it causes you to sin—"pluck it out." In case we didn't get the point, He added, "If your right hand offends you, cut it off." He didn't mean literally, but he wanted to emphasize that sin is an extremely serious matter. You can't play with sin; you must aggressively oppose it.

Do you have a sinful relationship? Cut it off. Are you looking at sinful images on your computer? Cut them off. Do you indulge in sinful passions? Cut them out. Eliminate them. Don't go down any street that causes you to stumble. Don't visit any place, don't patronize any restaurant, or stay in any office that consistently leads you into sin. If you can't stand against the temptations facing you in your job, then maybe you need a new job.

The Spirit must control our minds and wants us to mortify our flesh.

## LIVING BY FAITH

Galatians 2:20 summarizes the ideas in this entire passage well. Paul writes, "I have been crucified with Christ; it is no longer I who live, but

Christ lives in me; and the life which I now live in the flesh I live by faith in the Son of God, who loved me and gave Himself for me."

If you're not sure you're a child of God—if you've never trusted Jesus Christ as your personal Lord and Savior, and you're not sure that you would go to heaven if you died today—I would like to lead you in a prayer to invite Christ to come into your heart and be your Savior.

Repeat the following prayer, out loud, right where you are. Make it from your heart.

> *Dear Lord Jesus, I'm sorry for my sin. I ask You to forgive me, and come into my heart, and make me Your child. Fill me with Your Holy Spirit, and help me to live for You all the days of my life. I believe in You. I receive You as my Lord and Savior. In Jesus' name. Amen.*

If you prayed that prayer and meant it, God heard your prayer and has forgiven your sins.

God bless you, and welcome to the family of God!

4

# ADOPTED INTO GOD'S FAMILY

*For as many as are led by the Spirit of God, these are sons of God. For you did not receive the spirit of bondage again to fear, but you received the Spirit of adoption by whom we cry out, "Abba, Father." The Spirit Himself bears witness with our spirit that we are children of God, and if children, then heirs—heirs of God and joint heirs with Christ, if indeed we suffer with Him, that we may also be glorified together.*

*- Romans 8:14-17*

The apostle Paul stated in 2 Corinthians 5:17, "If anyone is in Christ, he is a new creation; old things have passed away; behold, all things have become new." In Romans 8, the apostle teaches us that as men and women "in Christ Jesus," we are part of the new creation.

We have a new relationship with God. We are sons and daughters of the Lord, born again into His family and adopted as His heirs. Don't get confused about the two pictures! We're not only born again into God's family—regenerated, given new life, and recipients of a new nature—but we are also adopted. The Bible uses both terms to describe what it means to be a Christian.

If someone asks, "Are you a Christian?" you can reply, "I'm born again, I've been adopted, my name is written down in the Book of Life, I'm a child of the King, I belong to Jesus Christ." God gave us every one of these descriptive terms to help us understand what it means to be "in Christ" and to have an eternal standing in Him as a beloved son or daughter.

The key theme in Romans 8:14-17 is sonship and heirship. By "sonship," Paul doesn't have in mind only men. "Sonship" means "adult children." The underlying Greek word translated "son" is *huios*, or "adult children of legal age." These sons and daughters enjoy all the blessings and benefits of true children of God. This relationship with God implies deep trust and intimacy.

God has become our loving Father.

In this passage, Paul gives us three blessings from the Holy Spirit that bring blessed assurance to the true believer. Let's condense all the doctrine in these verses (and there's a lot of it!) into these three descriptions of the work of the Holy Spirit in bringing assurance to the life of the believer.

## THE HOLY SPIRIT LEADS US

The first blessing is found in verse 14. Paul says, "For as many as are led by the Spirit of God...." In the original Greek, the words translated "led by" are in the present tense. It could be translated more literally, "being led by." Those who are being led by the Spirit of God ARE . . . .

There is no "maybe" here, or "might be," or "hope to be." The sons and daughters of God have an assurance, a certainty of being led by God. They have the standing of adult children. They will legally inherit *all* the blessings that come to believers as sons and daughters of God.

Do not miss this: ALL Christians are being led by the Holy Spirit.

If you are being led by the Spirit, then you're a son or daughter of God. They're inseparable; they're in one package. If you're God's child, then you are being led by the Spirit.

The apostle does not have in mind super saints, or a deeper life club - no! There are only two groups here: those led by the Spirit and those not led by the Spirit. I can't fully convey how important this is to understand.

Don't dismiss yourself and say, "Oh, well, I'm not one of those 'led by the Spirit' Christians.'" If you are a Christian, then you *are* led by the Spirit. *Every* Christian is being led by the Spirit. Don't be misled by speakers on television who make it sound as though they hear an audible voice from God every morning while brushing their teeth. Don't feel inferior! Don't feel second-class! God's Spirit IS in your life, and He is providentially, lovingly, and mercifully leading you.

Let's break this down a bit. What does it mean to be "led by the Spirit"?

- The Spirit renews our minds.

I'll never forget when I first got saved and became a Christian. I began to read the Bible with new eyes. I began to say, "This is awesome! God speaks!" The Bible became new and fresh.

Scripture tells us, "Do not be conformed to this world, but be transformed by the renewing of your mind" (Romans 12:2). The best way for your mind to be renewed and for the Spirit to lead you is to have the mind of God as expressed in the Word of God. The Spirit of God uses the Word of God to transform our minds.

- The Spirit stirs our hearts.

The Spirit renews our minds and stirs our hearts. To do what? To pray, praise, and proclaim. You get saved, and suddenly you say, "Wow! The Bible's *amazing*! God speaks to me through His Word!"

When you get saved, you start praying and talking to God. In verse 15 we cry, "Abba, Father," as we call to our Father in heaven.

I grew up in church, but not until I was born again did I really start to praise the Lord. I just kind of sat there, checking out the service. But the moment the Spirit came into my heart, He began to pluck the strings of my heart. I started singing with gusto to the Lord. I didn't say I sang well! But I sang to the Lord.

And then I began telling other people about Jesus.

It just happens.

We pray, praise the Lord, sing, and testify, all because the Spirit of God is in our hearts. God renews our minds and stirs our hearts.

- The Spirit directs our wills.

The Spirit directs our wills to live in holiness. When the Holy Spirit comes into your heart, if you start doing unholy things, He is grieved and quenched (Ephesians 4:30; 1 Thessalonians 5:19). He then convicts you. If you are a Christian and you step out of line, the Holy Spirit convicts you, shows you your sin, and directs you to repent and start living in a way that pleases God. The Spirit directs us all to yield to Him.

The Bible also tells us to "work out your own salvation with fear and trembling; for it is God Who works in you both to will and to do for His good pleasure" (Philippians 2:12-13). The Holy Spirit leads us to glorify God.

- The Spirit makes us God's sons and daughters.

The fact that God's Spirit leads you assures you that you are a son or daughter of God. And what does Paul mean by "sons of God"?

Remember that the word translated "sons" comes from the Greek term *huios*, which refers to a child mature enough to take on family privileges and responsibilities. The word "children" shows up in verse 16 as a very different Greek word (*technon*), one that means "born ones." Paul teaches us that we are both the adult sons and daughters of God *and* the children of God born by His Spirit.

No newborn human talks. Can you imagine being in the delivery room when your baby son is born, and a minute later, he says, "Hey, Dad and Mom. What's up? Good to see you. Let's go home!" You'd freak out. It takes time for that baby to develop.

My wife and I were in the kitchen one day, speaking on the phone with our youngest grandson, Hans. Hans was just starting to talk. I heard him say, "Papa." Awesome! My wife, Kristy, grabbed the phone and said, "Say, Nana."

"Papa," he said again.

I love it when our grandkids come running into my study and say, "Papa! Papa!"

When we become children of God, our hearts cry out, "Abba," or "Daddy!" Papa!

It takes infants some time to learn how to communicate. They don't immediately grow into it any more than we can drive a car right away. Only once we reach legal age do we start that process.

On the day I turned sixteen, I got my driver's license. Scary! I pulled out of the DMV and immediately ran into a post. I tore up the side of my dad's car. "Just keep going," Dad told me, "or they'll take away your license." I'll never forget that incident. I hadn't even gotten out of the DMV parking lot before I smashed my dad's car!

Once my father gave the keys back to me, I remember driving without an adult in the car. Wow! Do you remember that feeling? Freedom! My friends and I were driving in a car with no adults present. We could yell and scream and get crazy and do whatever we wanted to.

When you get even older, you might have an inheritance to claim. But in this country, you must be eighteen years of age to claim your inheritance.

It's very different when you're born into God's family. You don't have to grow and mature to enjoy the benefits of being God's child; you're immediately adopted. Your place as an adult child is to enjoy the benefits and blessings of talking to God, being led by God, being taught by God, and being used by God. The benefits and blessings are fully yours as a child of God.

## THE HOLY SPIRIT FREES US

Paul tells us, "For you did not receive the spirit of bondage again to fear, but you received the Spirit of adoption [the Holy Spirit] by whom we cry, 'Abba, Father'" (v. 15). God freed us from fear through the work of the Holy Spirit. Notice three tremendous facts about the Spirit freeing us.

1. We have not received "the spirit of bondage again to fear."

We are no longer slaves but sons. We're no longer under the bondage of the old law with its condemnation, sin, and death. We have a new liberty; we're freed. We've been given a new nature. We are the children of God who walk in the liberty whereby Christ has made us free. Therefore, we no longer live in bondage and fear.

2. We have received "the Spirit of adoption."

Paul clearly teaches the doctrine of adoption in this passage. From verses 14-17, Paul frequently makes references to "son," "children," or "heirs," all of them connected to our being children of God. Because we've been adopted, Paul says, we haven't received "the spirit of bondage again to fear."

Before we were saved, we lived in fear. But now, as sons and daughters, we don't have to fear. Why not? Because we've "received the Spirit of adoption." And what happens when we're adopted? We cry, "Abba, Father."

Only Paul uses the word "adoption" in the entire Bible. The Old Testament knows nothing of legal adoption. Adoption had a Roman origin, not a Jewish one, and Roman culture put a high priority on adoption.

A wealthy landowner who had no children might adopt a child or two, who would become his legal children with all rights to inherit their adopted father's estate. If a man had a natural-born son who was unworthy of receiving an inheritance, he might adopt another boy as his son, who *would* be worthy of that inheritance. That adopted son was just as legal as a biological child. Paul brought the glorious concept of adoption from the Roman culture into the New Testament.

Still, in the Old Testament, Moses became an "unofficially" adopted child. His mother, Jochebed, was forced to give him to Bithiah to raise as her own son. The Egyptian family of Pharaoh adopted Moses. In a similar way, Mordecai raised Esther, his younger cousin, as if she were his own daughter. Mephibosheth, the crippled son of Jonathan, the son of Saul, was unofficially "adopted" into the home of King David, as his "son."

I find it interesting that Saul was David's enemy, and like Mephibosheth, when God adopts us, we get transformed from enemies into children of God. Again like Mephibosheth, who was crippled in his legs, we're spiritually crippled and can't walk in the ways of God on our own. Mephibosheth sat at David's table and ate of the goodness of the king, and when God adopts us into His family, we enjoy great blessings from God the Father, God the Son, and God the Holy Spirit.

In Roman culture, adoption signified granting the full rights, privileges, and status of sonship in a new family, to which the adopted individual did not belong by nature. Likewise, you were regenerated when you became a Christian; God, in His power as the Creator, gave you new life. When you became a Christian, you were justified; God, as the judge, declared you righteous. And when you are adopted, God becomes your loving Father, and you are given all the rights, privileges, and responsibilities of a true son or daughter.

There is something sweet about adoption. Even though your biological children are a blessing, you don't get to pick them. You don't get to take them back to the hospital and say, "I'd like to exchange this one." You get whatever comes. Praise the Lord for that!

But when you adopt, you get to pick. As an adoptee, you're specially chosen. You get taken into the family and have the same rights as every other child. You become an heir and a joint heir with all the children in that family. It's exactly like that in the Christian faith.

3. We cry, "Abba, Father."

The Aramaic word "Abba" speaks of a close, intimate relationship between a father and his child. We would use the word "daddy" or "papa." When you become a Christian, you enjoy an intimate child-father relationship with God.

Jesus introduced this term into the Christian vocabulary. When He was in the garden of Gethsemane, praying in agony and sweating drops of blood, He said, "Abba, if it is possible, let this cup pass from Me; nevertheless, not as I will, but as You will." When He instructed us not to worry about what to eat or drink or wear, He told us, "Your Abba already knows what you need," and He will certainly provide it (Matthew 6:25-33).

I was blessed to have a loving earthly father. You might not have been privileged with such a dad; maybe you never even knew your biological father. But if you are a child of God, you have an Abba in heaven who loves you, cares about you, and has promised never to leave you or forsake you. He has promised to take care of you. He loves you more than anyone ever could.

We're free to rest in God's Abba love because we're led by the Spirit; we can look back over our lives and see how God led and guided us. I think of Psalm 23, where David said, "He makes me to lie down in green pastures. He leads me beside the still waters. Even though I walk through the valley of the shadow of death, I will fear no evil; for You are with me." God also tells each one of us, "You are My child." In prayer, we can say, "Abba, Father." God, who is infinitely high, is also intimately nigh. What an amazing truth!

## THE HOLY SPIRIT SPEAKS TO US

Not only does the Spirit lead us and free us, but the Spirit speaks to us. Paul tells us that *the Holy Spirit assures us* (v. 16).

The King James Bible says, "The Spirit itself," which is unfortunate because the Holy Spirit is not an "it." The Holy Spirit is a "He." Why, then, does the King James use the word "it"? It does so because in Greek, the word "spirit" is neuter, so translators chose the term "it." But in fact, the Holy Spirit is the third Person of the Trinity.

Jesus consistently used personal pronouns when speaking of the Holy Spirit. He said, for example, "He shall guide you" (John 16:13), "He will teach you all things" (John 14:26), and "He will testify of Me" (John 15:26).

The verse most accurately says, "The Spirit Himself bears witness [that's His work] with our spirit that we are children of God." Here, Jesus moves from the word *huios*, or "sons," to the word *techno*, or "born ones." We're reborn as children of God.

What a glorious reality! The Holy Spirit speaks to us and assures us. He bears witness with our spirit "that we are children of God" (v. 16). The Spirit of God gives us blessed assurance.

It always amazes me how many people say, "I can believe for other people, but I have a hard time believing for myself. I know other Christians are going to heaven, but I don't know if I'm going there." God does not want you to think any such thing! God wants you to have blessed assurance. He wants you to know that your sins have been forgiven and that you'll go to heaven to live with Him forever when you die.

In fact, you can start having heaven on earth *right now*. Someone once said, "A little faith will get your soul to heaven; a lot of faith will bring heaven to your soul." How glorious is that? There's no reason for any Christian to lack assurance, but maybe you lack assurance because you're not saved. Maybe you haven't been born again. If that's the case, I urge you to get saved today. Trust Jesus Christ and be forgiven of your sins!

But if you are a child of God, nothing could be worse than going through life biting your nails, fretting, anxious, and worrying about whether you're forgiven. God wants you to have blessed assurance. "God has given us eternal life," the Bible says, "and this life is in His Son. He who has the Son has life. These things I have written to you who believe in the name of the Son of God, that you may know that you have eternal life" (1 John 5:11-13).

Years ago, I learned an important lesson about the assurance of salvation that focuses on three areas. How do we know that we are saved?

1. We have the Word of God, the Father.

It's as simple as believing the Bible. God said it, I believe it, and that settles it. God, in His Word, said He has given us eternal life. That means that we are saved through faith in His Son, Jesus.

2. We have the work of God, the Son.

It's as simple as John 3:16: "God so loved the world that He gave His only begotten Son, that whoever believes in Him should not perish but have everlasting life." Do you believe that? If so, you're saved.

3. We have the witness of God, the Holy Spirit.

How does the Holy Spirit witness to us? According to Romans 8:14, He leads us. If you look back at your life, you can say, "God's never left me. He's always been with me." In my darkest, deepest moments when I've gone through the valley, God has always been there. I have sensed His presence.

The Holy Spirit also witnesses to us by putting a prayer in our hearts, in which we cry, "Abba, Father."

The Holy Spirit also speaks to us. We have the inner witness of the Holy Spirit. I realize that this last assurance is subjective. That's why the assurance starts with the Word of God the Father and the work of God the Son. Times may come when I don't "feel" saved. If you don't "feel" saved, you might not believe you *are* saved. But regardless of how you might feel, you can *know* you're saved because God says so in His Word.

Jesus died for you on the Cross. What a blessed assurance when the Holy Spirit comes to your heart and assures you that you are His child!

Do you have this inner witness today? As you sit there reading this book and reading His Word, do you have absolute assurance that when you die, you're going to go to heaven? If not, why not? God sent His Son to die on the Cross for your sins. If you reach out your hand with faith and trust in Jesus Christ, your sins can all be forgiven. No matter who you are or what you have done, *you* can be given new life, justified, and adopted into God's family.

As an heir of God myself, I can tell you that nothing's better.

## THE BENEFIT OF GOD'S BLESSED ASSURANCE

In the final verse of this passage, Paul does not describe another work of the Spirit to bring us assurance. Instead, he tells us how the assurance we've already heard about benefits us. He tells us the result of that assurance.

Because we are children of God, the Spirit leads us, frees us, and assures us. What happens, then? There are at least three results.

1. We're heirs of God and joint heirs with Christ.

2. We will suffer with Him.

3. We will be glorified together with Him.

These three benefits come from what Paul says in verse 17: We are "heirs of God and joint heirs with Christ, if indeed we suffer with Him, that we may also be glorified together."

All God's children will inherit the new heaven and the new earth. This world is not your home! You're just passin' through. "Your treasures are laid up beyond the blue," to quote a familiar song. That should excite you. You're not living just for your house, car, or bank account. You're not living only for the things that are seen but instead for the things that are unseen—and those things are eternal.

When the outlook is bad, try the uplook. That's what this verse is saying.

You have become an heir. You may not receive a great inheritance on earth that will set you up for life. But you're a child of the King! You're heir to the throne! You're heir to all that God owns!

One weekend, my wife and I drove to Monterey to see our kids. What a beautiful place that is—the coast, the mountains. It doesn't remind me much of Menifee, where our church is located. We trekked through pasture lands, farms, fields, and hills. As we drove, I thought, *I'm a child of the King. The cattle on those hills belong to my Dad. They're my Papa's. This beautiful coast with the waves crashing over the rocks also belongs to my Papa. And I'm going to inherit it all!*

We used to sing,

> A tent or a cottage, why should I care?
>
> He's building a palace for me over there;

Though exiled from home, yet still I may sing:

All glory to God, I'm a child of the King!

– Hattie E. Buell, "A child of the King"

We're heirs of God and one day will inherit everything He owns. Jesus says, "Come, you blessed of My Father, inherit the kingdom prepared for you from the foundation of the world" (Matthew 25:34). We'll inherit all things.

We're also joint heirs with Christ. If you're a legal child in a family, you have full legal standing along with all the other children. You're joint heirs along with them. So are we in God's family; we're joint heirs with our big brother, Jesus.

As God's sons and daughters, we identify with Him by suffering with Jesus. Most of us like the inheritance part a lot more than the suffering part. But Jesus Himself said that those who follow Him must pick up their cross and die to themselves (Matthew 16:24). Being a disciple, a child of God, means that we *will* suffer in this world. Suffering for Christ is the mark of a true Christian. Those who live righteously will suffer. Paul wrote elsewhere, "all who desire to live godly in Christ Jesus will suffer persecution" (2 Timothy 3:12).

Do you desire to live godly in Christ Jesus? If so, you should expect some trouble.

The end is not suffering, of course. One day, we will all be glorified together when our big brother, Jesus Christ, returns at the Second Coming. We will return with Him in power and glory and will become what the Bible calls "the manifest sons of God" (Romans 8:19). We will inherit all things. We will reign with Him for a thousand years (Revelation 20:6). We will enjoy "new heavens and a new earth in which righteousness dwells" (2 Peter 3:13).

Oh, how I pray that the truths of this text will sink deep into your heart!

If you're a Christian, a true child of God, you're being led by the Spirit. The Holy Spirit is reassuring you, leading you, and comforting you. What begins with God's grace will end in glory.

This is just where Paul wants to take us next.

## 5

# GROANING FOR GLORY

*For I consider that the sufferings of this present time are not worthy to be compared with the glory which shall be revealed in us. For the earnest expectation of the creation eagerly waits for the revealing of the sons of God. For the creation was subjected to futility, not willingly, but because of Him who subjected it in hope; because the creation itself also will be delivered from the bondage of corruption into the glorious liberty of the children of God. For we know that the whole creation groans and labors with birth pangs together until now. Not only that, but we also who have the firstfruits of the Spirit, even we ourselves groan within ourselves, eagerly waiting for the adoption, the redemption of our body. For we were saved in this hope, but hope that is seen is not hope; for why does one still hope for what he sees? But if we hope for what we do not see, we eagerly wait for it with perseverance. Likewise the Spirit also helps in our weaknesses. For we do not know what we should pray for as we ought, but the Spirit Himself makes intercession for us with groanings which cannot be uttered. Now He who searches the hearts knows what the mind of the Spirit is, because He makes intercession for the saints according to the will of God.*

*- Romans 8:18-27*

I'm a groaner. My wife says I groan too much, but I tell her it's biblical. In Romans 8:18-27, we hear a lot of groaning: from creation, Christians, and even the Holy Spirit. In this world, Jesus told us, we will have tribulation. But He quickly added, "Be of good cheer, for I have overcome the world" (John 16:33).

Yes, we suffer now, but we look in hope for the glory that's coming.

The older we get, the more artificial we become. We have artificial knees, artificial hips, artificial hair (or no hair), and artificial ears. I think, *John, you're so close to heaven; most of you is already there. There's not much left of you to go to heaven.*

As we get older, we groan more. I groan when I get up in the morning. I groan when I go to bed at night. Lately, I have had a hard time even bending over. *What am I going to do if something else breaks?* I ask myself.

I am groaning for glory.

When we became Christians, "all things passed away, and all things became new." We are new creations in Christ. We have a new position in Christ, without condemnation, a new life in the Spirit, and a new relationship with God as His children. We're heirs of God and joint heirs with Christ.

Nevertheless, even though we are God's children and share in His glory, in this world, we still suffer. Why? So that "we may also be glorified together" with Him. Both exist together: the theme of suffering and the theme of glory. Because we suffer, we groan—and what we groan for is glory.

So, if you're groaning today, you're being biblical. That's a scriptural thing to do.

## THE CREATION GROANS IN HOPE

The creation around us, the world we live in, is groaning for the hope of the liberty of the sons of God. Paul writes, "For I consider that the sufferings of this present time are not worthy to be compared with the glory which shall be revealed in us. For the earnest expectation [or "anxious longing"] of the creation eagerly waits for the revealing of the sons of God. For the creation was subjected to futility [or "vanity"], not willingly, but because of Him who subjected it in hope; because the creation itself also will be delivered from the bondage of corruption into the glorious liberty of the children of God. For we know that the whole creation groans and labors with birth pangs together until now" (vv. 18-22).

The surpassing greatness that awaits God's people is so great that it dwarfs, by comparison, the sufferings we go through now. Paul writes, "For I reckon...." The word "reckon" means "a fixed conclusion arrived at with careful consideration." It literally means "to think down upon." It carries the idea of a concentrated thought or of thinking deeply. It's used for the development of a mathematical equation.

I dislike math, and I'm not good at it. If I hear the word "math," I wig out, like I'm back in school. But in doing a mathematical equation, you bring it to its logical conclusion; that's what it means to think deeply, to concentrate. Paul says that he'd thought about this, looked deeply into it, and came to this conclusion.

Yes, we suffer in this world. If anyone tells you Christians don't have to suffer, don't listen to them because the idea isn't biblical. Live long enough, and trouble will find you. "Man is born to trouble, as the sparks fly upward," says Job 5:7. Something breaks, something goes wrong, something stops working. If you live in the world long enough, you will have heartache and suffer bereavement. You'll endure loss, suffering, and sickness.

But Jesus Christ brings us hope. Paul says that the sufferings we must endure on this earth don't begin to compare with the glory that will be revealed in us (v. 18).

But we're not in glory yet! We've had a taste of glory because the Spirit brings us that foretaste, but we're not home yet. We'll need to wait for the full glory. It "shall be revealed," however, when we go to heaven or when we're resurrected at the return of the Lord Jesus Christ. We don't see the glory now. We hold to it by faith; we believe in it.

Paul writes of our "earnest expectation" (v. 19) or the anxious longing of all creation. He's referring to the cosmos, to the created world, including both animate and inanimate things. He says the creation "eagerly waits for the revealing of the sons of God."

Paul must have thought about these things often, for he writes elsewhere, "our light affliction . . . is working for us a far more exceeding and eternal weight of glory" (2 Corinthians 4:17). If we should weigh out our suffering now and our glory then, the latter *far* exceeds the former. Our future glory will *enormously* outstrip our current suffering.

Interestingly, the apostle also says the created world will somehow share in our glory (v. 19). The creation itself eagerly awaits "for the revealing of the sons of God." What does that mean? We, as the sons of God, will be unveiled in all our glory when Jesus Christ returns to earth at His Second Coming. We will come back in our glorified, new bodies, and everyone will see that we are His children.

People today may not believe you are a child of God, but when you return with Jesus at the Second Coming, they'll say, "Wow!" You'll have a new, supernatural body, a new and improved you. No one will be able to argue the point then.

Many cult groups for years have tried to use this term, "sons of God," to describe themselves and their supposed deeper-life clubs. The term doesn't mean anything like that. Rather, it describes all Christians throughout the centuries. When they return with Christ at the Second Coming, everyone will see who the real "sons of God" are. Their return will foreshadow a glorious restoration of all creation.

## THE CREATION GROANS FOR GLORY

Paul then makes three statements about creation: its past, its future, and its present (vv. 20-22).

1. A statement about creation's past

Paul writes that the creation "was subjected to futility [or "emptiness"], not willingly, but because of Him [God the Father] who subjected it in hope" (v. 20). The apostle has in mind here the Fall when Adam and Eve sinned in the Garden of Eden, bringing the curse upon creation (Genesis 3). The world we live in, as beautiful and wonderful as it seems, is a fallen world.

Now, think about that. If the world we live in is as beautiful and wonderful as it appears—and it is fallen—can you imagine what it will be like when God turns it around and sets it on its right side? Can you imagine the beauty that awaits the children of God in that kingdom age when Jesus returns and ushers in a new heaven and a new earth?

When was creation made subject to futility? Genesis 3 tells us that Adam and Eve's sin brought a curse upon creation. God had put man over His creation, but man's sin meant that creation now suffers under the Fall. Sin brought earthquakes, tornadoes, hurricanes, tsunamis, and fires. Sin brought tragedy, death, and heinous crimes such as rape, murder, shootings, and genocide. We groan earnestly and ask God to come and set up His kingdom, our only hope. All of creation groans along with the believer.

The Fall brought emptiness and vanity. Man brought sin into God's creation against the will of the Creator. God permitted it to happen. But God has a purpose for allowing it, and ultimately a hope.

Have you ever looked back to the Garden of Eden before the Fall and thought, *Man, that would have been awesome!*? All the food you wanted? Just pick it from a tree, and no waiting in line to buy it —no credit cards. How amazing was that garden! God visited there during the cool of the day to walk with Adam and Eve (Genesis 3:8). Everything was spectacular.

We might want to say to Adam, "Why, oh why, did you eat the fruit? You *really* messed things up!"

In some sovereign, wise, divine way, God will one day reverse the curse. Man's story began in a garden, and the last book of the Bible tells us history will culminate in another garden (Revelation 22:1-3). But whatever we have to look forward to will be far greater and better than the original Garden of Eden.

God has designed history not only for our ultimate good but also for God's ultimate glory. Humankind fell, believers have been redeemed, and they will be lifted up all the way to a glorious experience of eternal bliss with God. Even though we feel sad as we observe the world around us, we can be glad that we have an amazing future and a hope: All of creation will be restored. A new world is coming!

2. A statement about creation's future

Paul writes that "the creation itself also will be delivered" (v. 21). Right now, creation is subject to vanity or emptiness. Ecclesiastes provides a biblical commentary on that idea. When you look at life without God, *all* is vanity, emptiness, and vexation of spirit. But the creation "will be delivered"! Creation has a great future, moving from the bondage of corruption into the glorious liberty of the children of God.

Theologians have called this teaching "Paul's cosmic soteriology." That's a fancy word for saying how God is going to save the universe. Not only does God save people, but He will also save the physical world. The cosmos will be restored at the "restitution of all things" (Acts 3:21).

Creation will be delivered, but not until the Second Coming of Jesus Christ. It won't happen when we elect a new president, or some favored party gets a majority in the House or the Senate. We won't have righteousness on earth until Jesus Christ comes back as King of kings and Lord of lords. He will set up His throne on the earth for a thousand years, a period called the Messianic age or the kingdom age. The Bible calls it a time of peace when righteousness will cover the earth as the waters cover the sea. And we will reign with Him. What a glorious time!

The nations of the world will "beat their swords into plowshares, and their spears into pruning hooks" (Isaiah 2:4). Wars and sickness will be things of the past. The lion will lay down with the lamb. And at the very end of history, there will be no more sin or death.

Creation groans for all of that.

Revelation 19 describes the Second Coming of Jesus Christ. Revelation 20 reveals how Satan will be bound by Christ for a thousand years. Think of it: A thousand years of no devil. That's awesome! At the end of the thousand years, Satan will be thrown into the lake of fire, where he will remain forever.

But until then, we suffer in this world.

3. A statement about creation's present

Paul wrote of creation's past in verse 20, its future in verse 21, and now its present in verse 22: "For we know that the whole creation groans and labors [or "travails"] with birth pangs together until now."

The word "travail" was used in Paul's day to describe the labor pains of a woman giving birth. Jesus used the same word when He spoke about the signs of the end of time. He called them "the beginning of sorrows" and mentioned earthquakes, famines, fires, and pestilence, as well as moral evils such as deception, persecution, and mass executions (Matthew 24).

If you have given birth to children, you know that the least enjoyable part of childbirth is labor. No woman ever says, "I don't really care about the baby; I just love going through labor." It's quite the opposite! Some of the most beautiful pictures I have of my wife were taken after the birth of one of our children when the baby was cleaned up and put in her arms. She glowed with joy because she had given birth to a new baby. If you had taken the picture fifteen minutes earlier, however, you would not call the photo "beautiful." No woman undergoing labor pains will say, "Take my picture." No. You wait until the baby is born; *then*, you can take her picture. You wait for her joy.

What God is doing in the cosmos involves travail and pain, while the Millennium is the birth of a new age. There is a new world coming! We must go through this time of travail, but soon, the creation will give birth to a new world. We look forward to that hope.

The Jewish day does not begin with the rising of the sun but with sunset. It then gets darker and darker until just before dawn, when it grows darkest. Only then does the dawn come. In a similar way, the world will get darker and darker until the dawning of a new age that will be introduced when Jesus Christ returns. So, although we live in suffering now (verse 17), we look for glory. Creation groans along with us.

As you watch the news and weep with those who weep and groan at all the discouraging events going on, creation groans with us. But never forget that although we live in a fallen world, Jesus has "overcome the world." Our hope is in Jesus.

## THE CHRISTIAN GROANS FOR GLORY

Not only does creation groan for glory, to be liberated from the curse, but the Christian also groans for glory. Paul says, "Not only that, but we [referring to Christians] also who have the firstfruits of the Spirit, even we ourselves groan within ourselves, eagerly waiting for the adoption, the redemption of our body. For we were saved in this hope, but hope that is seen is not hope; for why does one still hope for what he sees? But if we hope for what we do not see, we eagerly wait for it with perseverance" (vv. 23-25).

Remember two things when you interpret this section. First, this groaning comes out of the Christian. Paul is not talking about individuals outside of Christ. He's talking about Christians. *We* are groaning in hope. *We* groan for a future glory.

Christians groan for three reasons.

1. Christians groan because we have the Spirit.

Paul insists that we "who have [present possessive tense] the firstfruits of the Spirit, even we ourselves groan within ourselves" (v. 23).

The term "firstfruits" does not refer to the abundant fruity Christians out there. I once saw a bumper sticker that read, "God wants spiritual fruit, not religious nuts." There are a lot of fruitcake Christians, but Paul's not talking about them. He has in mind an Old Testament agricultural concept.

The term "firstfruits" refers to harvest time in the Old Testament when the Israelites gathered the harvest. Before they brought in the whole crop, they would harvest just a portion of their fields. That first portion, or "firstfruits," they consecrated or dedicated to God, something like a down payment on a house or a foretaste of what was to come.

Our family eats Thanksgiving dinner late in the afternoon. We get hungry before we eat, so many times I'll sneak into the kitchen when no one's watching to steal a sample. I'll taste a little turkey, stuffing, or mashed potatoes (my favorite). I take a bite and say, Hallelujah! Sweet! I can tell you, even before we have dinner, that it's going to be awesome because I've already tasted it.

That is exactly what the Holy Spirit does for you and me. I know heaven's going to be awesome because I've already tasted it. When we sing and worship the Lord, when we pray, when we feel His joy, peace, and love in our hearts, that's like a little sampling of heaven. The Holy Spirit is the firstfruits of our inheritance.

2. Christians groan because we're waiting for the redemption of our bodies.

Your body will be renewed. Paul writes, "We ourselves groan within ourselves, eagerly waiting for the adoption, the redemption of our body" (v. 23). As I've said, the older you get, the more you look forward to your new body.

"But I thought you said we already were adopted," someone objects. "What are you talking about when you say, 'waiting for the adoption, the redemption of our body'?"

Don't forget that salvation has three tenses: past, present, and future. We *have* been saved, we *are* being saved, and we *will* be saved. You won't understand the Bible if you don't understand this.

First, I've been saved—my sins have been forgiven. This is called "justification," where God declares us righteous. It's our position in Christ. Second, I'm being saved, present tense. This is called "sanctification," a lifelong process. I'm growing in the likeness of Jesus Christ. Third, I will be saved when I go to heaven and God gives me a new body. I will get that new, glorified body at the resurrection or the Rapture.

"But what if someone's cremated?" you may ask. Do you really think that's a problem for God? Do you think He says, "Oh, no! He shouldn't have done that. Bummer. What am I going to do now?" Believe me, it's no problem for God.

Do you know that "cemetery" literally means "resting place"? We lay our loved ones in Christ in a cemetery because we're waiting for the resurrection. I never stand in a cemetery and officiate a service without rejoicing that "the dead in Christ will rise first" (1 Thessalonians 4:16).

There will be a resurrection of our bodies, but for some who are yet alive and remain by the time the Lord comes, they "shall be caught up together . . . in the clouds to meet the Lord in the air" (1 Thessalonians 4:17). The Greek word *harpodzo* is often translated "caught up" or "snatched up." In Latin, the word was *rapturo*, from which we get our term "raptured."

So, whether you die and are buried, or if the Rapture happens before you die, you'll get a new, glorified body either way. By the way, if you're alive when the Lord comes back, you will be raptured. The Rapture involves the resurrection of the bodies of those who died in Christ and the "translation" of the living in Christ. Both scenarios represent the future hope of the believer. One way or another, we'll all get new bodies.

Paul likens our current body to a tent (2 Corinthians 5:1-2). He says that if our earthly body, "this tent, is destroyed, we have . . . a house not made with hands, eternal in the heavens. For in this we groan, earnestly desiring to be clothed with our habitation which is from heaven." We ache and groan in these bodies, but God will give us new bodies.

Elsewhere, the apostle writes, "So when this corruptible has put on incorruption, and this mortal has put on immortality, then shall be brought to pass the saying that is written: 'Death is swallowed up in victory. O Death, where is your sting? O Hades, where is your victory?'" (1 Corinthians 15:54).

Not long ago, we buried my father, at ninety-two years of age. We did so in hope and in anticipation of that resurrection day, when "the dead in Christ will rise first. Then we who are alive and remain shall be caught up together with them . . . to meet the Lord in the air."

I'm looking forward to that new body! The older I get and the more my tent leans, leaks, and flaps, the more eager I am to receive it. It's going to be glorious.

Jesus' resurrection body was a prototype of ours. You could see, touch, and hear Him, but He ascended back into heaven in that body.

In your new body, you'll never get sick or tired; you can always bend over; you'll never be out of breath, suffer from cancer or any disease, and never die again. Does that sound like anything you'd like to have?

That's the hope of the believer, but today, we groan because we want those new resurrection bodies.

> 3. Christians groan because we have hope that we're going to heaven.

Once you get to heaven, you'll no longer hope for heaven because you'll already be there. "For we were saved in this hope," Paul wrote, "but hope that is seen is not hope; for why does one still hope for what he sees?" (v.

24). He implies that we haven't seen heaven; we haven't gone to heaven; but we have hope for heaven. "But if we hope for what we do not see [heaven], we eagerly wait for it with perseverance [or "with patience"]" (v. 25.).

The New Living Translation of verse 24 says, "We were given this hope when we were saved." The moment you were born again, the hope of heaven came into your heart. Before then, you lived without God and without hope. What hope exists apart from God? What hope exists beyond the grave? Without God, how can anyone hope to see their deceased loved ones again? The only real hope lies in Jesus Christ—and the moment you were born again, you were born in hope and born unto hope.

As Christians, we have hope as a settled assurance. It's not wishful thinking or keeping your fingers crossed that Christianity is real, that there really is a God, and that heaven really exists. When you bury your loved ones, you need more than "I hope so." You need an assurance.

You need a blessed assurance.

The Bible says, "while we are absent from the body we are present with the Lord" (2 Corinthians 5:6) and "in His presence is fullness of joy; at God's right hand there are pleasures forevermore" (Psalm 16:11). One day we'll see our Christian loved ones and be reunited with them.

We are born unto hope. Christian hope, as defined in Scripture, is a settled assurance. Paul wrote that we have access by faith "into this grace in which we stand, and rejoice in hope of the glory of God" (Romans 5:2). We stand in God's grace, and we rejoice in the hope of God's glory. For good reason, Paul wrote of "Christ in you, the hope of glory" (Colossians 1:27). And because we have that hope, we look "for the blessed hope and glorious appearing of our great God and Savior Jesus Christ" (Titus 2:13). We look for His coming.

I love what Jesus said to His disciples: "You believe in God, believe also in Me. In My Father's house are many mansions . . . . I go to prepare a place for you. And if I go to prepare a place for you, I will come again and receive you to Myself; that where I am, there you may be also. Let not your heart be troubled, neither let it be afraid" (John 14:1-2, 27). Heaven is a real place, a prepared place. "The Father's house" refers to heaven, where the Lord has some special dwelling places waiting for us.

It's important that, as a Christian, you are heavenly minded, that you "set your mind on things above, not on things on the earth" (Colossians 3:2). Someone once said that "Hope is the measure of true Christianity." I emphasize this because much of popular Christianity today doesn't focus on heaven, sing of heaven, or even speak of heaven. It's all earthbound, focused on physical healing, wealth, and prosperity. Many say, "God wants you to be president of the bank," or "you're going to have a nice car and an amazing home." They speak all happy thoughts.

But what does Jesus say? "In the world you shall have tribulation; but be of good cheer, for I have overcome the world."

Is this just "pie in the sky in the sweet by and by"? I like my pie, but it's far from "just" that. Scripture doesn't mean you have no joy right now. We'll see in a bit that the Holy Spirit is our helper. It's better to be a Christian than not to be a Christian; as Christians, we have something great to look forward to.

What does a non-Christian have to look forward to? To grow old and die? And to leave it all behind? The Bible asks, "what will it profit a man if he gains the whole world, and loses his own soul?" (Mark 8:36). Where's your future? Where's your hope? What do you have to look forward to? What real joy do you have? It's so wonderful to know that I have a future and hope and that God has a purpose and a design for me.

Do you have such a hope? Do you know that when you die, you'll go to heaven? On what do you base your hope? We used to sing the song:

> My hope is built on nothing less
>
> than Jesus' blood and righteousness;
>
> I dare not trust the sweetest frame,
>
> gut wholly lean on Jesus' name.
>
> On Christ, the solid Rock, I stand;
>
> all other ground is sinking sand;
>
> all other ground is sinking sand.
>
> – Edward Mote, "My Hope is Built on Nothing Less"

If you don't have this kind of hope today, I urge you to find your living hope in Jesus Christ. And don't delay!

## THE SPIRIT GROANS TO HELP US

Creation groans for glory, Christians groan for glory, and the Comforter groans to help us. Paul writes, "Likewise the Spirit also helps in our weaknesses. For we do not know what we should pray for as we ought, but the Spirit Himself makes intercession for us with groanings which cannot be uttered" (v. 26).

Here, we have a reference to the Spirit groaning within us. As we wait in hope, we're not alone; we have the help of the Holy Spirit. It's not just that I get to go to heaven when I die, but that heaven has come to me *right now*. The Spirit has come to help me and be with me. The Holy Spirit is our helper. He comes alongside to help us.

The word "help" suggests looking at another person face-to-face and assisting that individual to pick up or hold something. For us, a good illustration might be picking up a couch.

I hate to move furniture. Who likes moving furniture? "We need that couch moved downstairs." Oh, great! "No, it doesn't look good right here. Take it back upstairs." Groan! When two people are moving a couch, there's no time for small talk. It's time to focus on carrying a big, heavy load.

That's what the word "helps" means here. It means the Holy Spirit is holding up His end of the weight. He's looking at you face-to-face and helping you to lift your burden.

You may have a financial burden, an emotional burden, or a physical burden. Perhaps your marriage is struggling, or you're having trouble with your kids. Maybe you've lost a loved one. Into that kind of tough situation, the Spirit comes and says, "Let me help you." And He picks up your burden with groans. He looks you right in the face as He carries His part of the load.

If you're a Christian, you have the Holy Spirit to help you. Whatever your burden or problem may be, let Him help you pick it up. Let Him help you bear your burdens. He wants to walk with you, talk to you, and be with you. *All* Christians have the Helper.

Why do we need Him? Because of "our weaknesses. For we do not know what we should pray for as we ought" (v. 26). Prayer is one of our weaknesses. We often have no idea how to pray or what to pray for. "But the Spirit Himself makes intercession for us with groanings which cannot be uttered. Now He who searches the hearts [God the Father] knows what the mind of the Spirit is," and the Spirit prays "according to the will of God" (v. 27).

God the Father, who searches all human hearts, also knows what is in the mind of the Spirit. The Spirit makes intercession for us in line with God's will. This is an interesting reference to "the mind of the Spirit," supporting the doctrine that He is a person. The Spirit has a mind.

When my father was alive, he was a man who knew how to pray. After he passed away, I received several calls and emails. Many of them said things like, "Pastor John, the way your Dad prayed, and to hear him pray, was *awesome*." My Dad was the only Christian I have ever met who would start to groan right in a prayer meeting. He would begin to cry. And you could sense the power and the work of the Holy Spirit in his life.

Do you know that this kind of groaning is an indication that you're a child of God? When the Spirit is in you, He'll groan. And so will you: "Lord, I need You! Lord, I want You! Lord, I can't wait to be with You! Lord, I need Your help! Lord, I need Your strength!" Sometimes, when prayer reaches its ultimate, words become impossible.

Many people pray with elegant words, but they have no heart. It's much better to have heart without words than words without heart. And it's infinitely better to have the Holy Spirit groan inside you.

## HOPE IS OURS

We live in a fallen world. We need to recognize that we will experience grief, tragedies, hurt and pain, loss and sickness, and sorrow. But there is hope in Jesus Christ!

Though the creation groans, it will be liberated. Though the Christian groans, every believer will get a new body and enjoy it fully in heaven. Though we often don't know what to pray for or how to pray, the Holy Spirit groans inside of us.

Hope is ours. And His name is Jesus Christ.

6

# GOD'S PROVIDENTIAL CARE

*And we know that all things work together for good to those who love God, to those who are the called according to His purpose.*

*- Romans 8:28*

Anyone who knows the Bible knows that Romans 8:28 is one of the all-time great verses of Scripture. It has been called the "soft pillow" for saints to rest their weary heads upon.

When you go through a time of suffering, sorrow, trouble, tribulation, or adversity, you can always turn to the promise of Romans 8:28, where you will read that "all things work together for good to those who love God, to those who are the called according to His purpose."

## A NEW KNOWLEDGE

Have you ever started a job and not finished it? When I was a teenager, I promised my dear mother that I would paint the house. I got the house half-painted and never finished it. My lapse still bothers me to this day. I should go back there and finish painting it, even though she's been in heaven for twenty years. When I get to heaven, I'll say, "Mom, I'm sorry I didn't finish that job."

You may start reading a book and fail to finish it, or you join the gym promising yourself to go every day, but you go only once—and you joined the gym three years ago. You may still say, "I'm a member of the gym," but you never visit it. You start many jobs, but you fail to finish.

Aren't you glad that God isn't like us? I am. God doesn't get tired of working in our lives. He doesn't say, "This John Miller is getting boring. I'm going to put him on the shelf and go on to someone else. I need to give up on him." No! Once God starts a work in our lives, God continues that work in our lives.

The great theologian Jonathan Edwards made a statement that I love. "What begins with grace," he said, "ends in glory." In other words, when God, in His grace, begins a work in your life, it is a sure thing that you will end in glory. God starts the process, and God will finish it.

As God's children, we not only have a new hope and a new help that comes to us from the Holy Spirit, but we also have a new knowledge. Yes, we know that we're going through times of suffering that will lead to glory (v. 18). But in this present suffering, we also can know something else. We can rest assured that God is working for our good and for His glory. That is why Paul wrote in Philippians 1:6, "and we know this very thing, that He who has begun a good work in you will complete it until the day of Jesus Christ."

Starting with verse 28, let's discover five facts about God's providential care. What do I mean by "providential care"? The word "providence" refers to God superintending our lives and watching over them. It speaks of God's provision, care, leading, and protection. It describes God's supernatural, sovereign protection, provision, and care of us.

## THE CERTAINTY OF GOD'S PROVIDENTIAL CARE

Verse 28 begins, "And we *know*...." This is the certainty. This is what I call the believer's blessed assurance.

It intrigues me that earlier, Paul spoke of something we don't know (v. 26b). We don't know how to pray or what we should pray for, so the Holy Spirit helps us in our weaknesses. In just two verses, we go from "we do not know" to "we know." Some things we don't know, while other things we do know.

From time to time, people say to me, "Pastor Miller, can I ask you a question?"

"Sure." When they ask their question, I sometimes have to say, "I don't know." And they looked shocked.

"Well, aren't you a pastor? Don't you get paid for answering deep, theological questions? Don't you have a red phone on your desk that you use to call God directly and get an answer to my problem?"

There is a *lot* we don't know. In the Christian life, God has chosen, in His wisdom, not to reveal certain things to us. The Bible says, "The secret things belong to the Lord" (Deuteronomy 29:29). Some things we won't know until we get to heaven. Only at that time will we see things clearly (1 Corinthians 13:12).

But thank God, other things we do know. When Jesus tried to wash Peter's feet at the Last Supper, Peter recoiled and said, "Lord, You're not going to wash *my* feet!" Jesus replied to him, "Peter, what I'm doing right now, you don't understand, but you'll know afterwards" (John 13:7).

I read that and think, *How fitting!* There is so much that God is doing in my life and your life that we don't understand. We don't understand why that loss, or why that bereavement, or why that heartache, or why that sickness, or why that job loss, or why that child has grown rebellious. But we will know hereafter; God has a plan, and we must rest in that plan.

How do we know? We know by faith. Did you notice that Paul doesn't say, "And we *see* that all things work together for good"? He doesn't say, "And we *feel* that all things work together for good." We often don't see, and we don't feel. "I don't feel God's presence. I don't see God working."

Someone said, "Many times the child of light must walk in darkness." When you walk in the darkness, never doubt what God spoke in the light. When you can't see, when you can't feel, and you don't understand, then rest in what you do understand: that "all things work together for good to those who love God, to those who are the called according to His purpose." Keep your focus on God.

Our translation of the passage doesn't insert the word "God" in this verse, but some manuscripts include it: "We know that *God* worketh all things to them who love Him and are called according to His purpose." Even if it doesn't explicitly appear in the text, the grammar implies that God is the one working. In our trials and troubles, therefore, we need to keep focused on God. I suggest you focus on three areas: God's person, God's promises, and God's power.

First, when you walk through a dark or difficult time, or you go through some adversity or suffer a loss and don't know what's going on, *rest on God's person*. He is a God of grace, love, mercy, and kindness. He is good all the time. He knows all things. He is everywhere present.

Second, we can rest on God's promises. God has given us "exceeding great and precious promises" in His Word. Discover the promises of God, claim them for your own, and fulfill whatever requirements they might have so you can live out His promises.

Sometimes, we make a promise but can't keep it. Maybe we didn't know the weather would turn bad. We didn't know the economy would turn bad. We didn't know the car would break down. We didn't know someone would get sick. We can't do what we promised because of circumstances beyond our control. But God always keeps His promises. Nothing lies outside of His control. That's why we can rest on God's promises.

Third, we can rely on God's power. Do you know that *nothing* lies outside of God's power? Nothing can thwart His purposes. What God has spoken cannot be broken.

The certainty of God's care for us means we can know *something*. We go through life not knowing a lot. But don't be discouraged because there are things we can know. Starting with this: "And we know that all things work together for good to those who love God, to those who are the called according to His purpose."

Someone put this truth in a poem:

> I know not where His islands lift
>
> Their fronded palms in air;
>
> I only know I cannot drift
>
> Beyond His love and care.

There is a lot I don't know, but I do know that "I cannot drift beyond His love and care."

## THE EXTENT OF HIS PROVIDENTIAL CARE

"And we know that *all things* work together . . . ." God's providential care extends to "all things." In the original Greek, the words "all things" means "all things." There are no qualifications or limits. Even bad things? Yes, even bad things.

And what is a bad thing? What is a good thing? In fact, what we call "bad" might actually be good, while what we call "good" might actually be bad. Let's allow God to determine what's bad and what's good.

Every event of our lives is included in this "all things." Good or bad remains under His loving, benevolent, sovereign control. This includes "the sufferings of this present time" (vv. 17, 18); it includes our groanings (v. 23); and it also includes our disappointments, our griefs, our illnesses, children who cause great pain, loss of wealth, loss or health, or lack of fruit in Christian service.

In His Sermon on the Mount, Jesus told us that when we feel discouraged or are going through hard times, we should become bird watchers. "Look at the birds of the air," He said, "for they neither sow nor reap nor gather into barns; yet your heavenly Father feeds them" (Matthew 6:26).

Many years ago, when I was going through a difficult time, I looked out on the front porch during a rainstorm. Huddled under the porch, I saw a little sparrow with a big, giant french fry in its beak. I think God created french fries just for birds. I have to buy french fries, but the birds get them for free. They just cruise down to their local fast-food place and scoop one up. This fry was bigger than the bird! He carried this huge thing in his beak.

Then I reminded myself of Jesus' words: *God, My Father feeds the birds. Are you not of more value than they? Not one sparrow falls to the ground apart from My Father knowing about it.* God attends the funeral of every sparrow—and you and I are of far more value than many birds.

Jesus also said, "Consider the lilies of the field . . . . They neither toil nor spin . . . yet even Solomon in all his glory was not arrayed like one of these." These gorgeous flowers bloom for one day and then get thrown into the fire. "Now if God so clothes the grass of the field, which today is, and tomorrow is thrown into the oven," Jesus continued, "will He not much more clothe you, O you of little faith?" (Matthew 6:28-30).

The answer is "Yes."

If you get discouraged, go outside. Study the birds, look at the flowers, and remind yourself that you have a Father in heaven who cares for you. Let your bird-watching lift your eyes to heaven.

## THE HARMONY OF HIS PROVIDENTIAL CARE

Every phrase in this verse is packed with truth: "And we know that all things *work together*"—not individually, but "together." God is working all things together. He's creating an amazing harmony in our lives.

William Barclay translates this verse, "We know that God intermingles all things for good for those who love Him."[4] In themselves, these things may not seem good. You may say, "Someone died. That's not good." Or someone else may say, "So-and-so has cancer. That's not good," or, "My friend went through a divorce. That's not good." But God can bring all those things together, working to harmonize them and use them for our good and His glory.

I don't bake cakes; I like to eat cakes. I don't know all the ingredients that go into a cake, but I've watched my wife and mom make a cake from scratch. They add flour, sugar, and eggs and then stir them all together. They put some other ingredients in there, too. They put the mixture in the oven, bake it, and out pops a beautiful cake.

My weakness is baked goods. I can smell or spot a bakery a thousand miles away. Every time I go into the store and see baked goods, I need to head the other way because I love that stuff.

If you took the individual ingredients of a cake and tried to eat them raw—eggs, sugar, flour—your mouth would revolt. It would taste terrible. But when you mix the ingredients in a bowl and put them in the oven, it becomes a beautiful cake. And that tastes good.

God takes your hurts, pains, joys, ups and downs, mountains and valleys, mixes them all together, and puts you in the oven. He's working to bring all those ingredients together for your good and His glory, to make something beautiful out of your life.

God works continuously, God works purposefully, and God works lovingly. God never stops working, and He always has a loving purpose. God is working all things in your life to create exquisite harmony.

## GOD'S PROVIDENTIAL CARE IS FOR *GOOD*

"And we know that all things work together *for good*." God works for our good and for His glory. And what is the ultimate "good" that God is working in our lives? God is working to make us like Jesus.

Once more, remember the three aspects of our salvation: past, present, and future. We *have been* justified (past tense). We *are being* sanctified (present tense). One day, we *will be* glorified (future tense). We have been made righteous, we are being made righteous, and we will be made fully righteous.

We are in the middle of that process now, in the present tense. We Christians have been forgiven, and we will be glorified, and right now, we're being sanctified. One of the chief means by which God sanctifies us is through suffering, trials, and hardships. He's trying to cut away things in our lives to make us more like Jesus. The goal of sanctification is Christlikeness. That is what God is trying to do in your heart and life and in mine.

While we'll look at this idea more in-depth in the next chapter, for now, briefly consider verse 29: "For whom [us] He [God] foreknew, He also predestined to be conformed to the image of His Son." God chose you, He determined what to do with you, and He's conforming you into the image of His Son. Why? "that He [Jesus] might be the firstborn among many brethren. Moreover, whom He predestined, these He also called; whom He called, these He also justified; and whom He justified, these He also glorified." It's a golden chain that cannot be broken. Whom God saves, He will glorify. What begins in grace will end in glory.

We must take care, however, to consider Romans 8:28 in its context. Everybody knows the verse and loves quoting it, but they often don't remember verses 29-30.

What is the good work that God is trying to do in my life? The good thing He is doing is trying to make me more like Jesus. I've heard this verse used for situations that don't fit its context. If my car breaks, for example, I might use the verse to assure me that I'm going to get a better one. If I lose my job, I might think this verse promises I'll get a better job.

But that's *not* what this verse teaches.

"Really, Pastor Miller?" someone says. "Why would you tell me that?"

I must be honest with you. If your car breaks, you might have to ride your bike to work for a while. Maybe God wants to humble you. Maybe God wants you to spend more time in prayer. Perhaps He wants to teach you something important; I don't know. But I *do* know that God works all things together for your good and for His glory. That doesn't mean that something great is going to happen right now! It means that God is trying to make you like Jesus Christ.

Oswald Sanders said, "Every adverse experience, when rightly received"—that's the key *when rightly received*—"can carry its quota of good. Bodily pain and weakness cause us to feel our frailty. Perplexity reveals our lack of wisdom. Financial reverses point out how limited our resources are. Mistakes and failures humble our pride. All these can be included in the term 'good.'"[5]

Oh, that we would look with that perspective! God wants to make every one of us into the image of His Son.

One of my favorite illustrations of this truth comes from 2 Corinthians 12, where Paul speaks of his "thorn in the flesh." The great apostle had a "messenger of Satan" that "buffeted" him. He prayed three times, asking God to take it away, but God said "No."

Because of the context, we understand what was happening. God had lifted Paul to heaven, where he saw astonishing visions and revelations. He understood things that no one else saw or heard. He came back to earth, saying it would be a crime for him to utter what he saw. And he added, "Because of the abundance of the revelations, there was given to me a thorn in the flesh, a messenger of Satan to buffet me, lest I be exalted above measure."

What was he given? A thorn.

Who gave it to him? God.

Because of the staggering blessings God gave to Paul, God also gave the apostle some burdens. Because of the apostle's paradise experience, God thought it necessary to give him a painful experience, too. God knows how to balance our lives.

The Lord continually reminds me that the infirmity and weakness of my flesh and the frailty of my life are His gifts to me to keep me humbly dependent upon Him. When we pray, "Take it away," God often says, "No; my grace is sufficient for you. My strength is made perfect in your weakness."

When Paul heard those words, he recognized that God was not going to take away this thorn—but he also realized that his Lord would give him His grace to bear his infirmities. Paul's weakness would become his strength. "Most gladly, therefore, I'll glory in my weakness," Paul responded, "for then the power of God will rest upon me."

What an example of how God lets sorrow, suffering, and weakness come into our lives to keep us humble and useable and to teach us that we need Him every hour!

While I do not know what you might be going through, I urge you to learn your lessons well. If you respond properly, God will use everything that happens to you for your good and for His glory.

## THE OBJECTS OF HIS PROVIDENTIAL CARE

"And we know that all things work together *to those who love God, to those who are the called according to His purpose*."

Notice that the text does *not* say, "All things work for good," period. People frequently misquote the verse. They leave it at "all things work together for good."

No, all things do not always work together for good. That's not a biblical idea. A person who wants to receive the promise that all things work together for good must meet two qualifications:

- The individual must love God.

- The individual must be called according to God's purpose.

If you want to claim this verse as a divine promise, you must meet its conditions. First, you must love God, which I believe is a reference to Christians. While it could refer to Christians who have a special love for God, I think it refers to all Christians. Second, those Christians must be called according to God's purpose. Let's unpack those two conditions a bit.

Deuteronomy 6:5 says, "You shall love the Lord your God with all your heart, with all your soul and with all your strength." This is the greatest commandment, the most important thing we can ever do. If we would focus our lives on loving God with all our heart, soul, strength, and mind, we'd see God taking care of us. Likewise, if we would love our neighbors as ourselves, we'd experience God taking care of us. We love God because He first loved us.

The second qualification is that we must be "the called according to His purpose." Our part is to love God; God's part is that He called us in eternity past. This calling reveals the sovereignty of God.

In this verse, therefore, we have man's part—loving God—and God's part—calling people to serve His purpose. We will take a deeper look at this issue in the next chapter. But for now, we must recognize that God calls us by His love and grace (vv. 29-30).

Do you know that you would not be a Christian if it were not for the love and grace of God? Do you know that God didn't choose you because you're intelligent? He didn't select you because of your good looks. He didn't choose you because you're charismatic, talented, or well-connected. God never said, "I really need that person on My team."

Much to the contrary, the Bible says that God "has chosen the foolish things of the world to put to shame the wise . . . the weak things of the world to put to shame the things that are mighty; and the base things of the world . . . and the things which are not, to bring to nothing the things that are, that no flesh should glory in His presence" (1 Corinthians 1:27, 28).

If God chose you, you are a candidate for His glory only because you're a foolish thing, a weak thing, a base thing, a despised thing. We were lost and living in darkness, but God, by His grace, came and rescued us.

The Bible gives us many examples of various difficulties and calamities working "together for good to those who love God." I think of the Old Testament story of Jacob. Joseph had vanished, Reuben had been disgraced, Judah was dishonored, Simeon and Levi had broken his heart, Dinah had been defiled, Simeon lay in prison, his beloved Rachael had died, and famine threatened the lives of his entire family. Then came a demand from Egypt that young Benjamin must also appear before the governor before the ruler would agree to release any further supplies.

Jacob began to weep. "You have bereaved me," he told his sons. "Joseph is no more, Simeon is no more, and you want to take Benjamin. All these things are against me" (Genesis 42:36).

I chuckle at his statement because I know what lies ahead in the next chapter. I want to shout, "Jacob, read the next chapter! Hang in there, buddy! Just turn the page of your life! You're all going to go down to Egypt. You will see Joseph there, alive, and well. He's gonna be there! All your kids will be there. God will provide!"

"All these things are against me," Jacob cried—but little did he know that "all these things" were working together by God for his good.

I also think of Joseph. Do you love the story of Joseph as much as I do? He was his father's favorite son, received a fancy coat that marked him out as his dad's special boy, became a hated outcast to his brothers, and was sold as a slave to Egypt. Talk about having a bad day! Try to imagine Joseph in a contemporary group therapy session.

"Joseph, what's your problem?"

"Man, all my brothers hate me, they threw me in a pit, they sold me as a slave to Egypt. I got here and this woman had eyes for me, but I did the right thing and resisted her. She lied about me and accused me of attempted rape, and I got thrown in this prison. I'm rotting here!"

But during all his troubles, Joseph never forgot God. Almost every time in his story, when we read of him speaking, he mentions God. God remained the center of his life. When finally Joseph was released from prison and slavery, after many years of suffering, he found himself sitting second to Pharaoh on the throne. Then, one day, all his brothers appeared before him. None of them recognized him, but he knew them right away.

You might think, *Man, he's really going to take vengeance on them now!* But Joseph told his brothers, "You meant it for evil, but God meant it for good" (Genesis 50:20). Isn't that amazing? Joseph looked at his brothers with tears running down his face and said, "Although you intended to harm me, God turned it around and used what you did to me for good."

God used Joseph to save many lives. God had a purpose for Joseph and a good plan for his life—and that good purpose and plan involved suffering.

Joseph's story foreshadows the ultimate picture of Romans 8:28, that of our Lord Jesus Christ. Although Jesus had done nothing wrong, He was rejected by men and crucified. Could anything be worse than sinful men crucifying the Son of God? God had come down from heaven, been born of a virgin, lived a sinless life, healed the sick, gave sight to the blind, raised the dead, fed the hungry . . . and hateful men took Him and nailed Him to a cruel cross.

The Crucifixion shows man at his worst but God at His best. On Calvary, love conquered hate, and goodness conquered anger.

Friends buried Jesus, but three days later, He rose from the dead. God took this horrible situation—the brutal execution of a righteous man who was also fully God—and used it to fulfill His plan. God put our sins on Jesus, Jesus atoned for our sins, and then our Lord rose from the dead. The Cross will forever stand as the ultimate picture of God working "all things together for good to those who love God and are the called according to His purpose."

## WE LOOK FROM THE UNDERSIDE

Have you ever read the book, *The Hiding Place*, by Corrie ten Boom? If you haven't, you should. It's the marvelous, true story of the Ten Boom family in Holland during World War II.

The Ten Booms made a secret place in their home to hide Jews from the Nazis. When they were discovered, Corrie's father and her sister, Betsie, were hauled off to prison. They both died there, while Corrie suffered in Ravensbrück Concentration Camp for many years.

The Ten Booms were Christians, children of God. They loved the Lord. Finally, God released Corrie from prison, and she began traveling the world to tell others about the goodness and mercy of God. Whenever she would speak, she would hold up the underside of a bookmark with a morass of strings and different colors of cloth that made no discernible pattern; it just looked like a mess. Later, she would turn over that bookmark to reveal the upper side, on which everyone could clearly see some beautiful, embroidered words that proclaimed, "God is love."

Corrie would remind her audience that in this world, we look from the underside. We see only a bunch of haphazard threads, dark and light, that make no pattern and seem to convey no message. From down here, we can't see or understand what God is doing.

But one day, we'll look from the upper side. And on that day, we will understand, without question, that God is love. It has been expressed in a poem titled "The Weaver."

> My life is but a weaving
>
> Between my God and me.
>
> I cannot choose the colours
>
> He weaveth steadily.

> Oft' times He weaveth sorrow;
>
> And I in foolish pride

Forget He sees the upper,
And I the underside.

Not 'til the loom is silent
And the shuttles cease to fly,
Will God unroll the canvas
And reveal the reason why.

The dark threads are as needful
In the weaver's skillful hand,
As the threads of gold and silver
In the pattern He has planned.

– Grant Colfax Tullar, "The Weaver"

We see only the underside, but one day, we'll see what God's design has been these many, long years. And on that day, we will joyfully shout, along with Joseph, "God meant it all for good."

## 7

# SALVATION'S GOLDEN CHAIN

*For those God foreknew he also predestined to be conformed to the image of his Son, that he might be the firstborn among many brothers and sisters. And those he predestined, he also called; those he called, he also justified; those he justified, he also glorified.*

*- Romans 8:29-30 NIV*

We're all familiar with Romans 8:28. We know it; we memorize it. We have that verse down pat. Our problem is that we don't carry it over into verses 29 and 30.

As wonderful as verse 28 is, verses 29 and 30 are even more wonderful because they tell us how God accomplishes our good and His glory. What is the "good" that God is working in verse 28? Verses 29 and 30 describe it.

Romans 8:29-30 has been called "the golden chain of five unbreakable links." In these five golden links, Paul traces God's saving purpose from eternity past to eternity future. It goes like this: our salvation started before time with the Father's foreknowledge, and it concludes, beyond time, in our glorification. In between those two, within time, comes our calling and our justification.

In this chapter, we'll investigate the five keywords that make the golden chain so unbreakable. Those five words are foreknowledge, predestined, calling, justification, and glorification. These words trace salvation's plan from eternity past to eternity future.

I realize this viewpoint can be controversial, but I'm not going to shy away from it. I won't water it down or try to avoid controversy. We're about to tackle head-on what I believe this text teaches us. I ask you to hear me out as you carefully consider these truths with an open mind. The authority lies in the Scriptures. When God speaks, we can rest assured that what He says is true.

## TWO IMPORTANT FEATURES

The salvation plan of God has two important features. First, *each link in the golden chain is made and fashioned by the hand of God*. I almost want to shout those words from the rooftops.

Everything we'll consider is what *God* has done and continues to do. This is about the work of God. So, praise and honor and glory be to God for His salvation! We do not and cannot save ourselves. It's all the work of God.

Most of us know quite well the declaration of Ephesians 2:8-9, "For by grace you have been saved through faith, and that not of yourselves; it is the gift of God, not of works, lest anyone should boast." We are saved *by* grace *through* the channel of our faith. But grace is a gift of God. Grace makes possible our salvation, which is also a gift of God. We cannot earn or deserve it, so we can't boast about receiving it.

Second, *each link in the chain is unbreakable*. God fashioned the links of the chain, which makes them unbreakable. What God has spoken cannot be broken. What God starts with grace will end in glory.

With that introduction, let's look together at each of the five links in this golden chain of God's salvation.

## LINK ONE: FOREKNOWLEDGE

Verse 29 says, "For those God *foreknew*...." What does God's foreknowledge mean? First, let me tell you what it does *not* mean.

It does not mean that God, knowing everything, looks forward and sees who is going to believe in Him, and with that knowledge, He chooses them based on their choice of Him. It does not mean that God looks down the corridors of time and knows, off in the distance, who is going to believe, who is going to receive, who is going to repent, and who is going to be saved, and based on that information, God elects those people.

People create this erroneous idea to "let God off the hook" and put salvation in man's court. But if this idea were true, it would eliminate the doctrine of election, so clearly taught in the Bible. Election insists that *God* chose *us*; we didn't choose Him.

Jesus said it plainly: "You did not choose Me, but I chose you" (John 15:16). None of us can completely comprehend this; we're baffled. Why would God choose *us*? *I* wouldn't have chosen me. Don't laugh; I probably wouldn't have chosen *you*, either. I don't know why God chose you, other than the fact that He chose the foolish things, the weak things, the despised things, the base things, "and the things which are not, to bring to nothing the things that are, that no flesh should glory in His presence"

(1 Corinthians 1:29). So, I'm a foolish thing, a weak thing, a despised thing. *That's* why God chose me.

God does not choose us based on our choice of Him. The Bible clearly does not teach any such idea.

What, then, does foreknowledge mean? The word in the Greek is *proginosko*, a compound term made up of two words: *pro* = "before" and *ginosko* = "knowledge." So, it means "before knowledge." It's a figure of speech, a kind of euphemism, a term that means more than just knowing something beforehand. It conveys the idea that salvation was initiated by God in His own eternal, loving choice. God knew you before, and God chose you.

Genesis 4:1 gives us an indication of how Paul used the idea in Romans 8. The Bible says, "Now Adam knew Eve, his wife, and she conceived and bore Cain." What does it mean that Adam "knew" his wife? The term refers to intimate knowledge; in this context, it speaks of a sexual relationship.

When the angel Gabriel visited Mary, he said to her, "Mary, you're going to have a baby, through the work of the Holy Spirit in you."

Mary asked, "How is this going to happen, since I have never been intimate with any man? How can *I* become pregnant?"

God chose Mary to be the mother of Jesus Christ. She didn't choose herself.

God set His love on us and chose us as objects of His loving purpose. God wants an intimate, deep, loving relationship with us. His "foreknowledge" refers to the fact that God set His love upon you, elected you, and chose you for salvation. Election is God's loving, gracious choice in salvation.

Ephesians 1:4 says, "He chose us in Him before the foundation of the world." Election is clearly taught in the Bible. God chose us before the foundation of the world. So yes, He knew us, but election means He set His love upon us and chose us to be His peculiar treasure.

The term is also used in 1 Peter 1:2, where Peter called Christians "elect according to the foreknowledge of God the Father." We are elect according to God the Father. He elected us and set His love upon us.

Some would say, "That's not fair! It's not right that God would pick just certain people." They get upset with God. I would balance this out by pointing out that this passage focuses on God's part, not our part. Our part is faith: we trust God and believe that we receive. That's not a work, that's not merited. We don't earn salvation.

John 3:16 says, "For God so loved the world that He gave His only begotten Son, that *whoever*...." This passage we're considering does not eliminate a "whoever" gospel. "WHOEVER believes in Him should not perish but have everlasting life."

"But what if God didn't choose me?" someone asks.

In that case, believe in Him. Then you'll become a "whoever."

"But how do I know I'm a 'whoever'?"

You believe to find out. You must trust Christ.

No one will ever be able to say, "I'm just not chosen." When you repent, believe that Jesus rose from the dead, and place your faith in Jesus for salvation, you'll find out He'll forgive your sins and give you eternal life.

It still amazes me that God chose *me*. I don't deserve it. I didn't earn it. I'm amazed that God would set His love upon me, that He foreknew me. That's where salvation began.

## LINK TWO: PREDESTINED

Verse 29 says, "For those God foreknew He also *predestined*." This word also causes people confusion, often along with some consternation. What does "predestined" mean?

First, it's *not* the same as "election." In election, God chooses you for salvation. "Predestination" comes from two Greek words, *pro* ("before") and *orizo* ("horizon"), so "before horizon." It means to "set off" or "designate." The word means "to decide beforehand" or "to mark out beforehand."

This word is never used for the unsaved. It is used only for the saved. Predestination is never for the unbeliever. God does not predestine anyone to go to hell. God didn't create people to fuel the fires of hell. He didn't create individuals and say that they can't be saved. The Bible says that God is "not willing that any should perish, but that all should come to repentance" (2 Peter 3:9).

Think about the word in English: "pre" (meaning "before") and "destination." The word means that even before God chose you, He decided what He would do with you. It's almost as if the Lord were saying, "Well, I've got him. What should I do with him?" And what is He going to do with us? He's going to conform us into the image of His Son, Jesus Christ. He does this so that Jesus Christ might be the Honored One, "the first begotten among the brethren."

What "good" things is God doing in our lives? Two things. First, we see salvation's purpose in verse 29. It says, "to be conformed to the image of His Son." Second, God wants to make Christ preeminent. Predestination means that God decided long ago to conform us to the image of His Son, that Jesus "might be the firstborn among many brothers and sisters."

God predetermined that one day, you and I will be like Jesus. That's good news! But we have a long way to go. We're not like Jesus yet.

Consider again that first purpose of salvation as described in verse 29: "For those God foreknew He also predestined to be conformed to the image of His Son." When will we be like Christ? It will happen when we die and go to heaven or when the Lord returns. And what does it mean to be like Christ? It means we will be like Him in both body and spirit.

One day, we will have the same kind of physical body that Jesus has in heaven right now. And what kind of body does Jesus have in heaven? The same body He had when He came out of the grave: a glorified, immortal, eternal body. That body can never get sick, has no weakness, and knows no pain. It'll be an awesome body! That body will be full of "glory," as we learned earlier in Romans 8. One day, it will be all yours. Forever.

If you're young, fit, and in good health, you may say, "No big deal." Just wait, buckaroo! In a few years, you'll be crying for a new body. The older you get, the more you groan for glory.

God put His love upon you, chose you, and beforehand determined your destination to one day be like Jesus. You'll have a glorified, immortal, eternal body. Elsewhere Paul tells us that God "will transform our lowly body that it may be conformed to His glorious body" (Philippians 3:21). John tells us, "we shall be like Him, for we shall see Him as He is" (1 John 3:2). The Bible declares that Jesus "has become the firstfruits of those who have fallen asleep" (1 Corinthians 15:20). While Christ is the most important Person who ever rose from the dead, we will follow in His resurrection and glory.

We also will be like Jesus spiritually. Salvation's purpose is for us to be conformed to Christ's image, both physically and spiritually. You will not have one iota, one trace, not even an ounce of sin. No more sickness, no more sorrow, no more tears—He'll wipe them all away.

If you're married, you know that your spouse isn't perfect. But that person to whom you're married, if he or she is a Christian, *will* one day be perfect. I know it's hard to imagine! One day, you will be perfect, too (and your spouse will have a hard time imagining *that*). You'll never lose your temper, and you'll never grow irritable; you'll never think a sinful thought or commit a sinful deed. You will be completely and utterly holy because He is holy.

Holiness involves all three tenses of salvation: past, present, and future. You are set apart and made holy positionally. You're being made holier throughout your time on earth. And one day, you will be perfectly, totally, completely holy once you're in the presence of our Lord, Jesus Christ.

The final and ultimate purpose of salvation is described to us at the end of verse 29. We are to make Christ preeminent: "that He [Jesus Christ] might be the firstborn among many brothers and sisters [referring to Christians]."

Paul calls us "brothers and sisters" to refer to the fact that Jesus is our big brother. Jesus is not only our Savior and Lord, but He's our big brother, and we're going to be part of Jesus in a marvelous way.

What does the apostle mean that Jesus "might be the firstborn among many brothers and sisters"? The Greek word translated as "firstborn" is *prototokos*. The Jewish world considered the firstborn son as the honored son. The firstborn got the inheritance. If you were the firstborn son in a family, you were the *prototokos*, the honored one, the elevated one.

When the Bible calls Jesus "the firstborn among many brothers and sisters," it means that Christ is the honored one, the venerated one. He is first in priority. He's first in importance. It means that Jesus Christ will be exalted among us.

Do you know that God devised salvation in such a way that Jesus gets all the glory, Jesus gets all the praise, and Jesus gets all the honor?

God the Father designed salvation in such a way that His Son would get a bride, the church. That bride will be holy, without blemish or spot. You and I are that bride, and we're going to be holy and without blemish or spot when we arrive in heaven. And then Jesus is going to take His bride and present her to the Father, that all things might be of God. It's a marvelous plan of salvation that Jesus would be exalted, that Jesus would get a bride, and that He would offer it back to God the Father in all praise to God.

The Bible says that Jesus Christ, "being in the form of God, did not consider it robbery to be equal with God, but made Himself of no reputation, taking the form of a bondservant, and coming in the likeness of men. Therefore, God also has highly exalted him and given Him the name, which is above every name, that at the name of Jesus every knee should bow...and that every tongue should confess...." (Philippians 2:6-11). That's what the text means when it says that Jesus would be "the firstborn among many brothers and sisters." Jesus will be honored as the exalted one, with a name "above every name."

Three times in Ephesians 1, Paul says that our salvation is "to the praise of the glory of His grace." This should humble us, not puff up our heads. Rightly understanding these truths should humble our hearts and give us a heart of gratitude. It should bring us assurance and foster in us a deeper love for God.

## LINK THREE: CALLED

Verse 30 says, "and those He predestined, He also *called*." All these things God did for us are spoken of in the past tense; they're a done deal. "Those He called, he also justified; those He justified, He also glorified."

At this point, we move from eternity past to present. This calling refers to God's gracious, direct appeal to our hearts. We respond in faith and are given the free offer of forgiveness and new life in Jesus Christ. The calling is God's application IN the time of His election, foreknowledge, and predestination BEFORE time. It comes to us through the preaching of the gospel. This is what we call the "general" or "universal" call.

Jesus stood up in the temple on a great feast day and said, "If anyone thirsts, let him come to Me and drink" (John 7:37-38). He really did mean "anyone." *Anyone* who is thirsty can come to Jesus and drink, and He will give them "living water."

I believe that in verse 30 Paul alludes to a second aspect of this call. It's an internal, specific, and effectual call. This is the work of the Holy Spirit in your life. You don't become a Christian unless the Spirit of God works in you. Some in church history have referred to Jesus as "The Hound of Heaven." He'll pursue you, follow you, convict you, convince you, break you, and bring you to a place where you finally say, "Lord, I surrender."

It happened to me the year I graduated from high school. Although I was raised in the church, I never surrendered my life to Jesus Christ. Out of nowhere—so it seemed, but now I know it came from heaven—the Holy Spirit came to me and said, "John, you're a sinner."

And I realized I was a sinner.

"John, you're going to hell."

And I realized I was going to go to hell.

"John, you need to get saved." Suddenly, I felt unhappy, miserable, and under conviction. God's Spirit started to draw me and draw me and draw me until I finally got hold of a Bible, started reading it, and began to pray and call out to God, repenting of my sins. At that moment, the

Holy Spirit flooded my heart with His joy, peace, and love. I felt a weight lift off my shoulders.

That was all the work of God's grace by the Holy Spirit. I didn't ask for it. I was going on my merry way when suddenly the Holy Spirit said to me, "Okay, John, now it's your time." And He reached out, grabbed hold of my life, and pulled me to Christ.

All of that is the work of the Holy Spirit. He regenerates you, gives you new life, and then indwells you. He "seals you for the day of redemption" (Ephesians 4:30) and then gives you strength and grace to live the Christian life. He opens the Scriptures to you and helps you to understand them. And then He transforms your life into the image of Jesus Christ.

It's all the work of God's Spirit. Salvation involves the Father, the Son, and the Holy Spirit. Your own calling happened when the Spirit of God came to you, convicted you, and convinced you that you are a sinner who needs Jesus. And then you surrendered your life to Him, trusted Him, and were saved.

I believe regeneration occurs the moment we believe in Christ, but it must be preceded by a work of conviction that draws us to Jesus. "No one can come to Me unless the Father who sent Me draws him," Jesus said (John 6:44). But He also said, "The one who comes to Me I will by no means cast out" (John 6:37). If you hear God knocking on the door of your heart, it's crucially important that you respond in faith.

## LINK FOUR: JUSTIFIED

"Those He called, He also *justified*." Like the call, justification happens in the present time. We go from eternity past—foreknowledge and predestination—to the present time—calling and justification.

When does justification happen? The moment the sinner believes in and trusts in Jesus Christ. What does justification mean? It means that God *declares* you righteous. Sanctification is the process God uses to make you righteous.

Justification is a forensic or legal term. It deals with your standing or your position in Christ. Romans 8:1 says, "There is therefore now no condemnation to those who are in Christ Jesus." Why not? Because in Christ, we are justified.

My favorite definition of justification is "the act of God whereby He declares the believing sinner to be righteous, based on the finished work of Jesus Christ on the Cross." All those whom God foreknows and predestines, He calls. And if you're called, then you're also justified. God called us, God saved us, and God justified us.

And how did He justify us? By grace alone, through faith alone, in Christ alone. Justification by faith alone is the theme of the whole book of Romans. It was the battle cry of the Protestant Reformation. We're saved by grace alone, through faith alone, in Christ alone.

Earlier in Romans, Paul had written, "being justified freely by His grace through the redemption that is in Christ Jesus" (3:24). The apostle says two things in that text: first, that we're justified freely by His grace, and second, that our redemption is in Christ Jesus. Four verses later, Paul writes, "Therefore we conclude that a man is justified by faith apart from the deeds of the law."

We are saved by grace alone, through faith alone, in Christ alone. We can't work for it. We don't deserve it. We can't merit it. If you have placed your faith in Jesus, you are justified. You're just and righteous before a holy God.

## LINK FIVE: GLORIFICATION

Glorification is the last link in this chain. "Those He justified, He also *glorified*" (v. 30). God foreknew, He predestined, He called, He justified, and then He glorified.

This means that what begins with God's grace in election ends with glory. Paul wrote, "being confident of this very thing, that He who has begun a good work in you will complete it until the day of Jesus Christ" (Philippians 1:6). Whenever God starts a work, God finishes that work.

It's important here to remember salvation's purpose: to make us like Jesus and bring glory and honor to Jesus. This glorification mentioned at the end of verse 30 accomplishes those two things. We receive a new body and get transformed into the image of Christ, and Jesus Christ gets all the praise, glory, and honor.

*That's* glorification. What begins with God's love and grace will end in glory.

## THE BIBLE IS CLEAR

I'm not so naive that I don't know Christians disagree on these issues. But I believe the Bible is perfectly clear. My authority is not church tradition. It's not denominational authority. Our authority is the Word of God alone. We stand on the Scriptures.

God sets His love on us. He predetermines what He's going to do with us. We'll arrive safely in heaven. He calls us in time, justifies us, and declares us righteous in our standing or position in Christ. One day, we'll be glorified in Him.

This passage is the greatest affirmation of assurance anywhere in the Bible.

Paul ends Romans 8 by saying that nothing "shall be able to separate us from the love of God which is in Christ Jesus our Lord." It opens with no condemnation, it ends with no separation, and in between is no defeat. How can we fail to give Him thanks, praise, and glory?

All of this is in the past tense. Grammatically, God foreknew us, He predestined us, He called us, He justified us, and He also glorified us—all in the past tense. The word "glorified" is even stronger in the Greek; it's in the aorist tense. That means it happened in the past, carries to the present, and takes us into the future. Verb tenses are critically important in this passage.

Jesus called Himself the Good Shepherd. In a parable, He told about the nature of the Good Shepherd; we learn that this shepherd started with 100 sheep and ended with 100 sheep. Aren't you glad that none of us will be missing when we get to heaven?

Can you imagine if that weren't true? "Where's Pastor Miller?"

"Oh, he slipped through My hands. Slippery little guy. I lost him."

Jesus told this parable about a Good Shepherd who had 100 sheep. One of them— a stubborn little sheep—went wandering off and got lost. If I were the shepherd, I'd say, "I have ninety-nine left; no biggie. I'm not going to endanger myself to find that one, little, stupid sheep." But Jesus is the Good Shepherd. He goes out, seeks for, and hears the frightened bleating of the lost sheep. He then finds the little rascal, puts it on His shoulders, and comes back rejoicing. He celebrates that this one little, lost sheep has been found.

Jesus begins with 100 sheep and ends with 100 sheep.

Jesus said it like this: "Of those whom you gave Me I have lost none" (John 18:9). And He prayed in John 17 like this: "Father, I desire that they also whom You gave Me may be with Me where I am, that they may behold My glory" (v. 24). Not only did Jesus pay the price for your sins, not only did Jesus make a promise to come again, but Jesus prayed a prayer asking God the Father that everyone who had been given to Him would end up with Him in glory. I believe that prayer will be answered! No wonder we sing,

> Blessed assurance, Jesus is mine!
>
> Oh, what a foretaste of glory divine!
>
> Heir of salvation, purchase of God,
>
> Born of His Spirit, washed in His blood.
>
> This my story, this is my song,
>
> Praising my Savior all the day long.
>
> – Fannie Crosby, "Blessed Assurance, Jesus is Mine!"

## OVERTAKEN BY GRACE

One of my favorite Bible teachers was Harry Allan Ironside, who pastored Moody Bible Church in Chicago for fifty years. He used to tell the story of a testimony meeting in which an older saint of God stood up and described how the Lord had sought him, saved him, given him the Spirit, protected him, and guided throughout his life.

In describing his conversion, he focused on all the things that God had done in saving him throughout his life. When the service ended, a younger, zealous, and more legalistic Christian approached the older man, desiring to correct him a bit.

He said, "I appreciated all you said about what God did for you. But you didn't mention anything about your part in it. Salvation is really part us and part God. You should have mentioned something about your part."

"Oh, yes," the older Christian said. "I apologize for that. I'm sorry. I really should have said something about my part. My part was running away, and his part was running after me until he caught me."[6]

That's the truth! You and I can take no credit for our salvation.

God gets all the glory.

Amen!

8

# BLESSED ASSURANCE

*What then shall we say to these things? If God is for us, who can be against us? He who did not spare His own Son, but delivered Him up for us all, how shall He not with Him also freely give us all things? Who shall bring a charge against God's elect? It is God who justifies. Who is he who condemns? It is Christ who died, and furthermore is also risen, who is even at the right hand of God, who also makes intercession for us. Who shall separate us from the love of Christ? Shall tribulation, or distress, or persecution, or famine, or nakedness, or peril, or sword? As it is written: "For Your sake we are killed all day long; We are accounted as sheep for the slaughter." Yet in all these things we are more than conquerors through Him who loved us. For I am persuaded that neither death nor life, nor angels nor principalities nor powers, nor things present nor things to come, nor height nor depth, nor any other created thing, shall be able to separate us from the love of God which is in Christ Jesus our Lord.*

*- Romans 8:31-39*

This final section of Romans 8 can rightfully be called "Blessed Assurance." We have a new life, a new relationship, new hope, new help, new knowledge, and a new assurance (verses 31-39). Some scholars have titled it "Paul's Hymn of Assurance."

It really is a song of assurance, building to the end of the chapter with a great crescendo: "Nor height, nor depth, nor any other created thing, shall be able to separate us from the love of God which is in Christ Jesus our Lord." Paul heartily sings this song and wants us to be assured of our salvation, too. It may be the most majestic passage in all the apostle Paul's writings.

This final passage opens in verse 31 with a question: "What then shall we say to these things?" Paul will employ six question marks throughout the passage, five of them used to answer this first question. His question refers to what he wrote in verses 28-30, where he told us that God has called us, justified us, and declared us righteous. And his answer is designed to bring the true believer blessed assurance.

This final section of Romans 8 is intended for one thing and one thing only: for true believers to be absolutely sure that one day they will arrive safely in heaven.

## THREE REASONS FOR ASSURANCE

This text gives us three reasons for our assurance. First, "*What then shall we say to these things?*"

What we say is that *God is for us* (verses 31-33). That's the first thing we say in response. "If God is for us, who can be against us?" Paul writes. Notice the question mark. Paul answers his question with a question.

"He who did not spare His own Son," the apostle continues, "but delivered Him up for us all, how shall He not with Him also freely give us all things?" (v. 32). The "all things" reference reminds us of Romans 8:28, where the apostle wrote, "*all things* work together for good to those who love God."

Paul wonders, "Who shall bring a charge against God's elect? It is God who justifies" (v. 33). As mentioned, Paul starts with a question and answers it with five more questions. We should memorize and take to heart all five of these important questions.

The first question comes in verse 31: "If God is for us, who can be against us?" The answer? No one. No one is greater than God.

Notice the word "if." This "if" does not question whether God is for us. In the Greek, it is an affirmation better translated as "since" or "because." It would then read, "Because God is for us...." Paul is *not* saying, "Oh, I hope God is for us." He's strongly affirming that *since* God is for us, no one can be against us.

Through his question, Paul declares our salvation secure. "Do you wonder if this salvation is real? If it can last? If you're going to arrive safely in heaven?" he's asking. "Do you wonder if God is really going to finish what He began in you?" And he answers, "God is for you. He's on your side. In fact, no one can ultimately be against you."

Because God is for us, no one can rob us of our salvation. To do so, they would have to be greater than God Himself, and no one is greater than God.

God is the giver, the sustainer, and the completer of our salvation. We sometimes lose sight of that fact. Salvation is of the Lord, and God sustains us by His grace. That's why we'll arrive safely one day in glory. We're saved by grace, we're kept by grace, and by God's grace, we will all arrive safely in heaven. We don't have to doubt whether that's so; we don't have to worry about it or fret about it. Whatever God starts, God completes.

Who is stronger than God? No one. David cried out, "The LORD is my light and my salvation; whom shall I fear? The LORD is the strength of my life; of whom shall I be afraid?" (Psalm 27:1). We don't need to fear anyone because God is for us.

And no one is greater than God.

Notice Paul's second question in verse 32: "He [God the Father] who did not spare His own Son, but delivered Him up for us all, *how shall He not with Him also freely give us all things?*"

The Old Testament gives us a picture of Christ's sacrifice in the account that describes the time God said to Abraham, "Take now your son, your only son Isaac, whom you love, and go to the land of Moriah, and offer him there as a burnt offering on one of the mountains of which I shall tell you" (Genesis 22:2). This is the first time the word "love" appears in the Bible. Here, it describes a father's deep love for his son. Abraham loved Isaac, but he desired to obey God even more.

Therefore, Abraham got up early one morning with Isaac, placed some wood on a donkey, and traveled together to the land of Moriah, where Jesus would be crucified on Calvary many centuries later. As father and son climbed the hill where the sacrifice was to take place, Isaac asked, "My father! Look, the fire and the wood, but where is the lamb for a burnt offering?" (Genesis 22:7).

Abraham replied, "My son, God will provide for Himself the lamb for a burnt offering" (Genesis 22:8).

There are two biblical ways to interpret that verse. It could be either "God Himself will provide a sacrifice"—He gave His Son—or "God Himself is the sacrifice"—for God was in Christ, reconciling the world to Himself. God not only provided the sacrifice, but God Himself was the sacrifice, as He was in Christ, reconciling the world to Himself.

Isaac voluntarily lay on the altar, and as his dad lifted the knife, ready to plunge it into the heart of his own son, God stopped Abraham and said to him, "Now I know that you fear God, since you have not withheld your son, your only son, from Me" (Genesis 22:12). At that moment, Abraham saw a ram caught in the bushes by his horns. Abraham took the ram, put it in the place of Isaac, and sacrificed it.

While Isaac did not die, God's own Son did die. Both stories picture the idea of substitution. The ram was the substitute for Isaac, even as Jesus was the substitute for us. Jesus took our sins, bore our griefs and sorrows, and died in our place. God gave His Son, Jesus, so Abraham did not have to sacrifice Isaac. But God did not spare giving up His only begotten Son.

The argument in Romans 8:32 moves from the greater to the lesser. Paul writes, "How shall He [God the Father] not with Him [the Son, Jesus Christ] also freely give us [His people] all things?" If God is willing to go all the way to give His Son to die for us on the Cross, then don't you think He will keep us, provide for us, protect us, and bring us safely home? If you ever wonder, *Does God love me? Is God going to take care of me?* Just look at the Cross. God is saying to us, "Never again question my love for you." It's an argument from the greater to the lesser.

Suppose that you go to a car dealership about to hold a raffle for a new car. You throw your name into the bucket, and a few weeks later, you get a call: "You just won a brand-new Maserati!"

"Great!" you reply. "I'll be right down!" You hurry down to pick up your car, which they give you, but they refuse to give you the keys.

"Are you kidding me?" you say. "You're going to give me the car, but you won't give me the keys?" That makes no sense.

The same form of argument appears here. If God would give you His only Son and sacrifice Him on the Cross for your sins, why wouldn't God now freely give you all things? Think of it as a blank check for the child of God. Whatever you need, God will meet that need. The Cross is God's guarantee of His unfailing love.

The third question asks, "Who shall bring a charge against God's elect?" (verse 33). Paul answers, "It is God who justifies."

Now, Paul takes us into a courtroom. He could have said, "Who will charge us?" and we could have answered, "The world; others will come against us. The flesh; my own heart will condemn me."

Has your own heart ever condemned you? Maybe as you're getting ready to go to church one morning, you hear, "Who do you think you are, going to church? You're not a good Christian; you've been sinning so much lately that you're not worthy. Everyone else at that church is holier than you. You don't deserve to go to church! Who do you think you are?" Your heart and your flesh condemn you.

The devil is also very good at condemning you. He is "the accuser of the brethren" (Revelation 12:10). Remember how he appeared before God to point his finger at Job? When God bragged about Job, Satan answered that Job served God only because God had blessed Job. But if God were to take away those blessings, Satan predicted Job would surely curse God to His face.

The world, the flesh, and the devil will all come against us, but God Himself has declared us righteous. God is not against us; He is for us. God gave His Son to die for us, and He is the one who justifies us. To be justified means that God declares you righteous.

So, when you come into the courtroom as God sits on the bench, remember that He's your heavenly Father and has already declared you righteous. You also have a good defense attorney—Jesus Himself. It just so happens that the judge is His Father! Jesus goes up to the judge and says, "Dad, everything's cool with this guy. I know he's kind of flakey, but he trusted Me. He's one of ours, so justify him."

The gavel comes down, and the judge says, "I declare this man to be righteous." That's our position or standing before God. "Whom He called," remember, "these He also justified." If you are a Christian, you have been declared perfectly, totally righteous before God. God sees you as though you have never sinned. He doesn't condemn you; He's the one who has justified you.

So, rest in God's purpose and God's power! And rest assured that God is for you.

Paul then gives a second response to the question, "What then shall we say to these things?" It comes in verse 34: "Who is he who condemns? It is Christ who died, and furthermore is also risen, who is even at the right hand of God, who also makes intercession for us." God the Father is for us, and God the Son died for us.

The fourth question also appears in verse 34: "Who is he who condemns?" It is certainly not Jesus; He is the one who died for you. It's certainly not God the Father; He's the one who is for us.

Three realities in verse 34 assure us of our salvation. Each is critically important:

- Jesus died for you
- Jesus rose for you
- Jesus intercedes for you.

The verse says, "It is Christ who died, and furthermore is also risen, who is even at the right hand of God, who also makes intercession for us."

"Christ who died" refers to Jesus' crucifixion on the Cross, where He took our sins. He didn't die on the Cross merely to say, "I love you." He died there to pay the penalty for your sins.

"Christ . . . is also risen" refers to Jesus' resurrection from the dead. Jesus died for you, and three days later, He rose for you. The Resurrection provides proof that the price Jesus paid on the Cross was accepted by the Father as a complete atoning sacrifice for your sins. When Jesus hung on the Cross, He cried, "It is finished (*tetelestai*)," which means "finished" or "complete." Then He dismissed His spirit and died. He was buried, and three days later, God the Father said, "Amen" to Jesus and raised His Son from the dead.

Paul wrote that Jesus was "declared *to be* the Son of God with power according to the Spirit of holiness, by the resurrection from the dead" (Romans 1:4). Christ's resurrection is God the Father's stamp of approval on Jesus' work on the Cross. How can we know that what Jesus did on the Cross really paid for our sins? We know because God the Father raised Him from the dead—*that* was the divine validation and proof.

The text, "Christ . . . is even at the right hand of God, who also makes intercession for us," refers to Jesus' ascension and exaltation. He rose from the dead and ascended into heaven, where He continues to intercede for us. We often miss this work of Christ. We are very good at looking back at the Cross and remembering the price Jesus paid on the Cross, that He died, was buried, rose again, and returned to heaven—but what is Jesus doing *now*? Jesus is praying for you. He is interceding for you. He is right there by the Father as your advocate. He lives to intercede for you (Hebrews 7:25).

Remember when Jesus turned to Peter and said, "Satan has asked for you, that he may sift you as wheat"? (Luke 22:31). Can you imagine Jesus turning to *you* and saying, "Hey, Satan called Me last night. He said that he wants you."

"What did you tell him? You didn't tell him 'Yes,' did you?"

Do you know that Satan wants you? That the devil wants to sift you? He wants to ruin your marriage, ruin your witness, ruin your joy, and your love and make you of no effect for Christ. He wants to rob you of all the blessings of your Christian life. He can't steal your salvation; this whole passage makes that clear. However, he can certainly try to take away your joy and peace. He certainly can work to nullify your witness. Satan desires to "sift you as wheat."

But Jesus said to Peter, "I have prayed for you...and when you have returned to Me, strengthen your brethren." In part, Peter did this very thing by writing First and Second Peter.

Satan also wants to "sift *you* as wheat." But Jesus sits at the right hand of the Father, praying and interceding for you. He keeps busy praying for you every day. What a blessing!

The book of Hebrews talks about Jesus, the High Priest who lives to make intercession for us. He can be touched by the feelings of our infirmities and weaknesses. He was tempted in all points as we are, yet He never sinned. God empathizes with us, sympathizes with us, and is compassionate toward us. He *understands*. We have a big brother in heaven, so to speak, who sits at the right hand of God the Father, continually interceding for us.

How can we be sure of our salvation? Let me give you a formula I learned years ago that I have always remembered. You can use it as a foundation for your own assurance. First, *Jesus paid the price*. Second, *Jesus prayed a prayer*. And third, *Jesus made a promise*.

Jesus *paid the price* by dying for our sins on the Cross. Never doubt your salvation! It was paid in full by Jesus on the Cross.

Jesus *prayed a prayer* to intercede for us. "Father," He said, "I desire that they also whom You gave Me [referring to us, His people] may be with Me where I am, that they may behold My glory" (John 17:24). What a great prayer! Jesus asked His Father, while still on earth, that everyone whom the Father had given Him would be with Him forever. Jesus wanted us to see His glory. God the Father *will* answer that prayer of God the Son, and we'll be with Him in heaven to see it answered.

Jesus *made a promise* in John 14:1-3, where He said, "Let not your heart be troubled; you believe in God, believe also in Me. In My Father's house are many mansions; if it were not so, I would have told you. I go to prepare a place for you. And if I go and prepare a place for you, I will come again and receive you to Myself; that where I am, there you may be also." Jesus promised He would go to heaven and prepare a place for us.

Heaven is a real place, a prepared place. Heaven is the Father's house. And one day, Jesus is going to return and take us, either by death or by the Rapture. We're going to heaven to live with Him forever.

Those three things are the foundation for your assurance. So, rest in the Son of God's perfect sacrifice, in the sufficiency of His finished work, and in His continual advocacy as He intercedes for us at the right hand of the Father, praying for us.

## NOTHING CAN SEPARATE US FROM GOD'S LOVE

The third response to Paul's question, "What then shall we say to these things?" is this: Nothing can separate us from the love of God in Christ Jesus.

Paul makes his general question more explicit in this final question: "Who shall separate us from the love of Christ? Shall tribulation, or distress, or persecution, or famine, or nakedness, or peril, or sword? As it is written:

'For Your sake we are killed all day long; we are accounted as sheep for the slaughter.'"

That's quite a question! And the apostle has quite an answer: "Yet in all these things we are more than conquerors through Him who loved us. For I am persuaded that neither death nor life, nor angels nor principalities nor powers, nor things present nor things to come, nor height nor depth, nor any other created thing, shall be able to separate us from the love of God which is in Christ Jesus our Lord" (Romans 8:37-39).

You should clap for that one. *Nothing* can separate you from His love.

First, God is for you. Second, Jesus died for you. And third, nothing can separate you from the love of God. *Nothing*.

Paul scans heaven and earth and makes it very clear that NOTHING can separate us from God's love. The Father is for us, the Son died for us, and God the Holy Spirit regenerates and indwells us, baptizes us, and seals us unto the day of redemption. God will never, *ever* leave us.

Please understand that something amazing happened to you when you became a Christian. It started with regeneration, the work of the Holy Spirit. He made you alive and new in Christ. We use the term "born again," but the technical term is "regenerated." A Christian is someone who has the life of God in his or her soul. You're not a Christian because you go to church, believe in God, or read the Bible; you're a Christian because God's life has come into your soul. That's what makes you a Christian. It's called being born again, the work of the Holy Spirit (John 3).

The Holy Spirit also indwells every believer. Every Christian has been regenerated and is being indwelt by the Holy Spirit. The Holy Spirit comes to live inside you. Your body becomes the temple of the Holy Spirit. Once He moves in, He will never leave.

Third, the Holy Spirit baptizes us by taking us out of Adam and placing us in Jesus Christ, who is called "the last Adam." The Spirit takes us out of darkness and translates us into light. He takes us from bondage and sets us free. Every Christian has been baptized by the Holy Spirit; it's the work that identifies you with Christ.

Romans 8:1 tells us we are "in Christ Jesus." Romans 8:39 tells us we are "in Christ Jesus." How did you get in Christ Jesus? By the Holy Spirit. The moment you were regenerated and indwelt, you were taken out of Adam and placed into Christ. Once in Christ, always in Christ.

You did not put yourself in Christ, and you cannot take yourself out of Christ. You didn't save yourself, and you can't lose your salvation or keep yourself saved. Your salvation is kept by the power of God. Once you are in Christ, once you are indwelt, once you have been regenerated, you can never be lost. You can't be unregenerated or unregenerate yourself. You can't take yourself out of Christ and go back into Adam. You can't get the Holy Spirit to leave; He will "never leave you nor forsake you."

The Holy Spirit also seals us: "And do not grieve the Holy Spirit of God, by whom you were sealed for the day of redemption" (Ephesians 4:30). The number one image and concept in the sealing of the Holy Spirit is security, not ownership. While sealing does convey ownership, its primary function is to convey your security.

People in the ancient world sealed their letters. Some of us continue that practice today. We place a wax seal on the envelope or send it by secure post. In the ancient world, only two people could break that seal: the sender and the receiver.

In salvation, God is both the sender and the receiver, which means only He can break the seal. If you are a Christian, then you have been sealed by the Holy Spirit until the day of redemption, until you get safely to heaven.

Therefore, "He who has begun a good work in you will complete it until the day of Jesus Christ" (Philippians 1:6).

Paul asks, "Who shall separate us from the love of Christ? Shall tribulation, or distress, or persecution, or famine, or nakedness, or peril, or sword?"

"Tribulation" means to be pressed by affliction or hardship. The word "distress" means a difficult, tight place; you feel hemmed in and can't get out. "Persecution" comes for Christ's sake. People oppose you because of your faith. "Famine" means a lack of supplies or food. "Nakedness" means a lack of clothing or provision. The word "peril" refers to any kind of danger. Have you ever been in danger? Not even that can separate you from God's love. The Greek word translated "sword" referred to a short dagger, not a long sword. It's the same sort of sword that Peter pulled out in the Garden of Gethsemane, which he used to try to take off Malchus' ear (John 18:10). It gives us a word picture for death; "sword" implies death. Not even death can separate us from God's love! Even when you die, you will be more than a conqueror.

Paul suffered from each of these things. He suffered tribulation, distress, persecution, famine, nakedness, and peril. Not long after he wrote these words, he would be executed for his faith. I find it interesting that Paul wrote to the Christians in Rome. In Rome, Emperor Nero would soon begin to kill Christians. The very recipients of this letter would soon be thrown into the arena and devoured by wild beasts. They would be covered with pitch, put up on a pole, lit on fire, and used as human torches. Paul, too, would be executed for his faith.

Nowhere does the Bible promise to exempt us from suffering and sorrow. In fact, quite the opposite. Scripture recalls the stories of many believers who suffered great problems and persecution, who "wandered about in sheepskins and goatskins, being destitute, afflicted" (Hebrews 11:37). Not everyone will be delivered in this life. Many times, God allows us to go through these trials.

Romans 8:36 quotes Psalm 44:22: "For Your sake we are killed all day long; we are accounted as sheep for the slaughter." Paul quotes the Septuagint version of the Old Testament, a widespread Greek translation. David wrote this psalm about what a life of faith can look like.

When was the last time you heard someone preach on this text? We're killed all day long; we're like sheep about to be slaughtered. We suffer adversity and difficulty—but none of it can ever, in the least, affect our relationship with God or separate us from God's love.

Paul continues in verse 37, "Yet in all these things we are more than conquerors." Yes, we're like sheep headed for slaughter; but even *then*, we are more than conquerors? What on earth could that mean?

How can someone be "more" than a conqueror? Isn't conquering enough? The word literally means "super conqueror." It's like winning a sports event and saying, "we super won the game."

"What do you mean? Didn't you just win the game?"

"Yes, we won, but we killed 'em! We slaughtered 'em!"

When Paul looks at you as a believer in Christ, he says that you're not merely a conqueror; you're a super conqueror. You're an over-conqueror. You're a super conqueror "through Him who loved us." The word "love" appears in the aorist tense there and refers to the Cross. In the past, Jesus loved us by dying for us, and His action carries on into the present and the future. In and through Jesus Christ, we are more than conquerors.

## THE GREAT CRESCENDO

Paul's conclusion reaches a crescendo in verses 38-39, where he starts, "For I am persuaded." The word "persuaded" means that he has "absolute assurance" or "confidence." So, he has ultimate assurance. About what?

Paul is persuaded that "that neither death nor life [whether he lives or dies] nor angels [good angels, who have no reason to separate us from God's love] nor principalities nor powers [evil angels, fallen angels or demons] nor things present [nothing happening in your life right now] nor things to come [even your future is secure] nor height nor depth [not even space itself] nor any other created thing [he scans the entire universe for any little, green men on a planet out there somewhere] shall be able to separate us from the love of God which is in Christ Jesus our Lord."

How marvelous is *that*?

Now you can see why I called this book *Blessed Assurance*. Romans 8 opens with no condemnation and ends with no separation. And in the middle, "All things work together for good to those who love God, to those who are the called according to His purpose." Because we are in Christ, we can never be separated from God's love.

## AND STILL, THERE IS MORE

Paul didn't come up with this amazing message on his own. Jesus Himself had said, "My sheep hear My voice, and I know them, and they follow Me. And I give them eternal life, and they shall never perish; neither shall anyone snatch them out of My hand. My Father, who has given them to Me, is greater than all; and no one is able to snatch them out of My Father's hand" (John 10:27-29).

Who gives these "sheep" eternal life? Jesus. How long does eternal life last? Forever. So then, if God gives you eternal life, how long are you going to live?

Eternally.

Why do we argue about this? Why do we debate this in church? "I give them eternal life," Jesus says. Eternal life is eternal. If you don't live eternally, then you never had eternal life. If you don't have eternal life, then you won't live eternally. The term refers to both quality and quantity. It's a new life that lasts forever. It's not intermittent eternal life: now you have it, now you don't, now you've got it again. No, it's ETERNAL.

Jesus also says, "They shall never perish." Did He need to say that? Couldn't He just have said, "I give them eternal life"? Wouldn't that be enough? Apparently not, so He adds to it: "They shall never perish."

And then He adds a third element: "Neither shall anyone snatch them out of My hand. My Father, who has given them to me, is greater than all." Paul clearly had learned this lesson well, for he wrote, "If God is for us, who can be against us?" Jesus insists that God is for us, and therefore, "no one is able to snatch them out of My Father's hand."

Someone might ask, "but what if I snatch myself out of His hand?" Then you need to ask yourself a question: "Am I greater than Jesus' Father, the Creator of the Universe?" I think the answer is obvious. And you should ask yourself a second question: "What does 'no one' mean?" It means no person, no being, no entity. If you are a person, a being, or an entity, then you also have no power to snatch yourself out of the Father's hand.

If you belong to Christ, then your salvation story begins with no condemnation and ends with no separation. Really, though, your story will never end.

It's eternal.

## A CLOSING DOXOLOGY

Jude closes his little book with a magnificent doxology, and I'd like to borrow his words to close this book. Jude writes,

> *Now to Him who is able to keep you from stumbling, and to present you faultless before the presence of His glory with exceeding joy, to God our Savior, who alone is wise, be glory and majesty, dominion and power, both now and forever. Amen (verses 24-25).*

God is for us, Jesus died for us, and NOTHING can separate us from the love of God, which is in Christ Jesus.

And *that* is the ultimate Blessed Assurance.

# NOTES


1. Barnhouse, Donald Grey, *Romans, Vol 7: God's Heirs: Exposition of Bible Doctrines* (United Kingdom: Wm. B. Eerdmans Publishing Company, 2023), p. 2

2. Morris, Henry M. *The Genesis Record* (Grand Rapids: Baker Book House, 1976), p. 181-182.

3. Graham, Billy, *The Holy Spirit: Activating God's Power in Your Life* (United Kingdom: Thomas Nelson, 2011), p. ix

4. Barclay, William, *The Letter to the Romans* (United Kingdom: Saint Andrew Press, 1957), p. 116

5. Sanders, J. Oswald, *Spiritual Maturity: Principles of Spiritual Growth for Every Believer* (United States: Moody Publishers, 2007), p. 17

6. Boice, James Montgomery, *To the Glory of God: A 40-Day Devotional on the Book of Romans* (United States: Baker Publishing Group, 2010), p. 100

# More resources by Pastor John Miller

Through the Bible, God reveals Himself to us. It's His divine autobiography, centered on Jesus Christ and inspired by the Holy Spirit. This living and powerful Word unveils answers to life's profound questions and provides the essentials to living the Christian life. Pastor John Miller presents five vital topics every believer and Bible student should understand:

- God and the Bible
- Jesus and the Bible
- The Holy Spirit and the Bible
- The Church and the Bible
- The Christian and the Bible

Available at revival.tv

MARRIAGE
AND THE BIBLE
John Miller

www.ingramcontent.com/pod-product-compliance
Lightning Source LLC
LaVergne TN
LVHW010947110826
845149LV00015B/3237

* 9 7 9 8 9 9 6 0 2 1 6 0 4 *